TALI SHAROT is the author of *The Optimism Bias* and a professor of cognitive neuroscience with degrees in economics and psychology. She is the founder and director of the Affective Brain Lab at University College London. Her papers on decision-making, emotion, and influence have been published in *Nature*, *Science*, *Nature Neuroscience*, and *Psychological Science*, among many others. She has been featured in numerous outlets and has written for *The New York Times*, *Time* magazine, *The Washington Post*, CNN, and the BBC, among others. Before becoming a neuroscientist, Sharot worked in the financial industry for a few years and completed her national mandatory service in the Israeli air force. She lives in London and Boston with her husband and children.

ALSO BY TALI SHAROT

The Optimism Bias

Additional Praise for *The Influential Mind*

"Packed with practical insights, this profound book will change your life. An instant classic." —Cass R. Sunstein, Harvard University; former administrator, White House Office of Information and Regulatory Affairs; and bestselling coauthor of *Nudge*

"Take it from a leading neuroscientist: every day, we all miss opportunities to influence others. This timely, intriguing book explains why it's so difficult to shift the attitudes and actions of others—and what we can do about it." —Adam Grant, *New York Times* bestselling author of *Originals* and *Give and Take*

"It not only demonstrates the failings of the human mind to learn from our mistakes—for instance, resorting to fear-mongering—but carries a practical series of lessons in overcoming those habits. And those habits, are everywhere we look. . . . Beyond the tricks of mind influence, there is a great deal of promising news in the book, about what we as humans value." —*Wired* (UK)

"Lucid and engaging . . . Sharot's treatment is particularly valuable for its balance between accessibility to the reader and solid grounding in scientific research. In today's 'post-truth' environment, her efforts to increase awareness of the pitfalls of human reasoning, and how to overcome them, are an indispensable contribution from the coalface of cognitive scientific research." —*Science*

"In the arena of behavioral science, little has held more potential than the striking advances in behavioral neuroscience, and little has stood to gain as much from those advances as the study of social influence. With

The Influential Mind, Tali Sharot has offered an account that makes the connection in a way that is both instructive and engaging."

—ROBERT B. CIALDINI, author of *Influence* and *Pre-Suasion*

"Better facts tend to be counterproductive on hot-button issues like gun control. As Tali Sharot notes in her book *The Influential Mind* . . . the smarter a person is, the greater his or her ability to rationalize and reinterpret discordant information, and the greater the polarizing boomerang effect is likely to be." —DAVID BROOKS, *The New York Times*

"In the age of big data, it's easy to assume that cold, hard facts can drive change. Not so fast, argues cognitive scientist Tali Sharot, whose new book, *The Influential Mind*, explores how emotion tends to overpower reason when it comes to human decision-making." —TIME.com

"In every chapter of this book about social psychology, its neuroscientist author manages an insightful and discomforting observation about the human mind. She challenges some common ideas (warning about the wisdom of crowds, for instance), while reinforcing others (that we are not good natural statisticians). And it's illustrated with good examples. Her section on how instant feedback changes behavior will leave you wondering about people's unwashed hands in every restaurant or GP surgery you visit."

—*The Times* (One of Six Best Political Books of 2017)

"This book is not only a primer on persuasion; it is far more valuable than that. It explains why so many of our well-meaning attempts to change people's minds can backfire so badly."

—RORY SUTHERLAND, vice chairman of Ogilvy & Mather

"Readers will discern plenty of ways to sharpen their abilities to carry an argument. [Sharot] questions the prevailing 'wisdom of the crowd,' strength-in-numbers folderol of recent business and pop-psych books. . . . To put it less nicely than she does, the human herd mentality can make us jump on any number of misguided bandwagons. Feel free to think politics there, and Sharot has some useful tips on how to prevail in political arguments by working the priors—i.e., 'building on common ground instead of trying to prove others wrong.'" —*Kirkus Reviews*

"A fantastic journey through the process of forming beliefs and ideas."
—Tony Hsieh, CEO of Zappos.com and
New York Times bestselling author of *Delivering Happiness*

"[A] fascinating, accessible primer on what current research teaches us about the art of persuasion. Her book strives to 'reveal the systematic mistakes we make when we attempt to change minds,' a topic that resonates in today's divisive political climate. . . . She has a gift for providing engaging vignettes that are apt and illustrative for nonacademics. The writing exhibits model clarity and brisk pacing. Readers will find themselves jotting notes to apply Sharot's findings to a wide range of areas, including workplace politics, parenting, and Facebook arguments." —*Publishers Weekly*

"In this perceptive study, cognitive neuroscientist Tali Sharot isolates seven factors central to influence." —*Nature*

"*The Influential Mind* brilliantly unpacks the science of influence, offering guidance not only on how to influence others—but how to stop others from influencing us." —Michael Norton, Harvard Business School, coauthor of *Happy Money: The Science of Happier Spending*

"Sharot smartly pairs findings based in neuropsychology with those derived from behavioral psychology to illustrate how one field builds upon another. . . . Sharot's target audience is the general public, not specialized professionals, but her presentation of numerous interdisciplinary findings in psychology, behavioral economics, and neurobiology lends her book nuance and sophistication. . . . [She] has a lot to teach us about our power to change others." —*Psychotherapy Networker*

"Concisely written, compellingly presented, and eminently applicable."
—STEVE MARTIN, *New York Times* bestselling
coauthor of *Yes!: 60 Secrets from the Science of Persuasion*

"Another timely read, *The Influential Mind* is a book that will help you understand how persuasion works, and why it so frequently doesn't. Along the way neuroscientist Tali Sharot knocks down some clichéd assumptions (e.g. "the wisdom of crowds"—guess what, the crowd isn't always so wise), reveals why some tendencies prevail despite all efforts (e.g. willing embrace of ignorance over embrace of knowledge), and provides a few clues as to how we can be better persuaders in our everyday lives (e.g. it's occasionally valuable to know how to persuade your boss). A readable, grounded book that's on point for our era of persuasion." —*Forbes* (A Must-Read Brain Book of 2017)

"This brilliant and timely book is essential reading for anyone who wants an intelligent, principled guide to getting their ideas heard and their hopes fulfilled. If you follow Tali Sharot's science-backed guidance, you'll become one of those great communicators and changemakers that everyone raves about—persuasive and inspirational in equal measure." —CAROLINE WEBB, author of *How to Have a Good Day*,
CEO of Sevenshift, senior adviser to McKinsey & Company

"With a scientist's vision and a writer's grace, Sharot unmasks the secrets of influence: how people make and change their minds—and why."

—David Eagleman, Stanford University neuroscientist
and *New York Times* bestselling author

The Influential Mind

What the Brain
Reveals About Our Power
to Change Others

TALI SHAROT

PICADOR

HENRY HOLT AND COMPANY

NEW YORK

THE INFLUENTIAL MIND. Copyright © 2017 by Tali Sharot. All rights reserved. Printed in the United States of America. For information, address Picador, 175 Fifth Avenue, New York, N.Y. 10010.

picadorusa.com • instagram.com/picador
twitter.com/picadorusa • facebook.com/picadorusa

Picador® is a U.S. registered trademark and is used by Macmillan Publishing Group, LLC, under license from Pan Books Limited.

For book club information, please visit facebook.com/picadorbookclub or email marketing@picadorusa.com.

Illustrations on pages 32, 50, 58, 63, 72, 98, 107, 143, 160, 177, 186, 191, 201 by Lisa Marie Brennan, lisa@saber.net

Designed by Meryl Sussman Levavi

The Library of Congress has cataloged the Henry Holt edition as follows:

Names: Sharot, Tali, author.
Title: The influential mind : what the brain reveals about our power to change others / Tali Sharot.
Description: First edition. | New York : Henry Holt and Company, [2017] | Includes bibliographical references.
Identifiers: LCCN 2016058450 | ISBN 9781627792653 (hardcover) | ISBN 9781627792660 (ebook)
Subjects: LCSH: Influence (psychology) | Social influence. | Attitude change. | Neuropsychology.
Classification: LCC BF774 .S53 2017 | DDC 158.2—dc23
LC record available at https://lccn.loc.gov/2016058450

Picador Paperback ISBN 978-1-250-15961-8

Our books may be purchased in bulk for promotional, educational, or business use. Please contact your local bookseller or the Macmillan Corporate and Premium Sales Department at 1-800-221-7945, extension 5442, or by email at MacmillanSpecialMarkets@macmillan.com.

First published by Henry Holt and Company, LLC

First Picador Edition: September 2018

10 9 8 7 6 5 4 3

For Josh

Contents

—◆◆◆—

Prologue

---◈---

A Horse-Sized Syringe

The Surprising, Baffling, Mysterious Case of Influence

You and I share a role. Maybe you never stopped to consider this role, or perhaps you think about it all the time. If you're someone's spouse, parent, or friend, you fulfill this role. If you're a doctor, teacher, financial adviser, journalist, manager, or human being—you fulfill it.

This duty we all share is to affect others. We teach our children, guide our patients, advise our clients, help our friends, and inform our online followers. We do this because we each have unique experiences, knowledge, and skills that others may not. But how good are we at this role?

It seems to me that the people with the most important message, those who have the most useful advice, are not necessarily the ones who have the largest impact. Recent history is full of such puzzles, from the entrepreneur who convinced investors to pour billions into a shaky biotech endeavor to the politician who failed to convince citizens to fight for the future of their planet. What, then, determines whether you affect the way others think or whether you are ignored? And what determines whether others change what you believe in and how you behave?

The underlying assumption of this book is that your brain makes you who you are. Every thought that ever crossed your mind, every feeling you ever experienced, every decision you ever made—was all generated by neurons firing within it. Yet your very own brain, on the top of your neck, is not fully yours. It is the product of a code that has been written, rewritten, and edited for millions of years. By understanding that code, and why it is written the way it is, we will be better able to predict people's reactions and understand why some common approaches to persuasion often fail while others succeed.

For the past two decades, I have been studying human behavior in the lab. My colleagues and I have conducted dozens of experiments in an attempt to figure out what causes people to change their decisions, update their beliefs, and rewrite their memories. We systematically manipulated incentives, emotions, context, and social environments and then peered into people's brains, recorded their bodily responses, and documented their behavior. It turns out that what most of us believe will cause others to alter their thoughts and actions is wrong. My aim with this book is to reveal the systematic mistakes we make when we attempt to change minds, as well as to illuminate what occurs during those instances in which we succeed.

I am going to begin in my own backyard, with the story of how I was almost persuaded to ignore years of scientific training by a man whose unexpected influence on millions has baffled many.

* * *

On the evening of September 16, 2015, at around eight p.m., I was sitting on the sofa in my living room watching the second Republican primary debate on CNN. The 2016 presidential race was one of the most interesting in history, full of unexpected plot twists and surprises. It also turned out to be a mesmerizing study of human nature.

Center stage at the Ronald Reagan Presidential Library, in Simi Valley, California, were two of the leading candidates: pediatric neurosurgeon Ben Carson and real estate mogul Donald Trump. In between discussions about immigration and taxes, the debate turned to autism.

"Dr. Carson," began the moderator, "Donald Trump has publicly and repeatedly linked vaccines, childhood vaccines, to autism, which, as you know, the medical community adamantly disputes. You're a pediatric neurosurgeon. Should Mr. Trump stop saying this?"

"Well, let me put it this way," replied Dr. Carson. "There have been numerous studies, and they have not demonstrated that there is any correlation between vaccinations and autism."

"Should he stop saying that vaccines cause autism?" asked the moderator.

"I've just explained it to him. He can read about it if he wants to. I think he's an intelligent man and will make the correct decision after getting the real facts," said Dr. Carson.

While I did not always agree with Dr. Carson, I did concur with him on this issue. I happened to be familiar with the literature, not only because of my profession as a neuroscientist but also because I'm the parent of two young children, who at the time were two and a half years old and seven weeks old. So I was utterly surprised by my reaction to what Trump said next.

"I'd like to respond," said Trump. "Autism has become an epidemic. . . . It has gotten totally out of control. . . . You take this little beautiful baby, and you pump—I mean, it looks just like it's meant for a horse, not for a child. And we've had so many instances, people that work for me. Just the other day, two years old, two and a half years old, a child, a beautiful child, went to have the vaccine, and came back, and a week later got a tremendous fever, got very, very sick, now is autistic."[1]

My response was immediate and visceral. An image of a nurse inserting a horse-sized syringe into my tiny baby emerged inside my head and would not fade away. It did not matter that I knew perfectly well that the syringe used for immunization was a normal size—I panicked.

"Oh, no," I thought. "What if my child gets ill?" The fact that these thoughts were running through my mind shocked me. Nevertheless, anxiety, a feeling all too familiar to parents of all beliefs and backgrounds, abruptly took over.

"But, you know," said Dr. Carson, "the fact of the matter is, we have extremely well-documented proof that there's no autism associated with vaccinations."

No matter. Proof, shmoof. Dr. Carson could have cited a hundred studies, and it would have had no effect on the storm that erupted inside my head. I was absorbed by that stallion of a needle that was about to cause my child to get very, very ill.

It made no sense. At one podium was a pediatric neurosurgeon whose ammunition included peer-reviewed medical studies and years of clinical practice; at the other was a businessman whose arguments boiled down to a single observation and intuition. Yet despite my years of scientific training, I was convinced by the latter. Why?

I knew exactly why. And it was that understanding that brought me back to reality.

While Carson was targeting the "cerebral" part of me, Trump

was aiming at the rest of me. And he was doing it by the book—this book.

Trump tapped into my very human need for control and my fear of losing it. He gave me an example of someone else's mistake and induced emotion, which helped align the pattern of activity in my brain with his, making it more likely that I would take on his point of view. Finally, he warned of the dire consequences of not following his advice. As I'll explain in this book, inducing fear is often a weak approach to persuasion; in fact, in most cases, inducing hope is more powerful. However, under two conditions, fear works well: (a) when what you are trying to induce is *in*action and (b) when the person in front of you is already anxious. These two criteria were satisfied in this case, as Trump was lobbying against the act of immunization, and his target audience—new parents—are the poster children for stress.

The fact that I understood how Trump was affecting my thoughts subsequently enabled me to pause and reevaluate the situation; I would not change my mind on this issue—my young son will receive immunizations, just as my daughter did before him. But I wondered how many other new parents out there were persuaded by his arguments. I also pondered what would have happened if Dr. Carson had done a better job of addressing people's needs, desires, motivations, and emotions, rather than assuming that they would make the correct decision after receiving the facts.* Dr. Carson was speaking to millions, and he missed an extraordinary opportunity to make a difference. We all encounter such opportunities. You may not routinely address millions, but you address people every day: at home, at work, online, offline.

---

* A study I describe in chapter 1 reveals why Dr. Carson's approach was likely to fail and what he could have done instead.

The fact of the matter is that people love propagating information and sharing opinions. You can see this clearly online: every single day, four million new blogs are written, eighty million new Instagram photos are uploaded, and 616 million new tweets are released into cyberspace. That is 7,130 tweets per second. Behind every tweet, blog, and uploaded photo is a human being like you and me. Why do millions of humans spend millions of precious moments every day sharing information?

It appears that the opportunity to impart your knowledge to others is internally rewarding. A study conducted at Harvard University found that people were willing to forgo money so that their opinions would be broadcast to others.[2] Now, we are not talking about well-crafted insights here. These were people's opinions regarding mundane issues, like whether Barack Obama enjoys winter sports and if coffee is better than tea. A brain-imaging scan showed that when people received the opportunity to communicate their pearls of wisdom to others, their brain's reward center was strongly activated. We experience a burst of pleasure when we share our thoughts, and this drives us to communicate. It is a nifty feature of our brain, because it ensures that knowledge, experience, and ideas do not get buried with the person who first had them, and that as a society we benefit from the products of many minds.

Of course, in order for that to happen, merely sharing is not enough. We need to cause a reaction—what Steve Jobs aptly referred to as making a "dent in the universe." Each time we share our opinions and knowledge, it is with the intention of impacting others. The intended change can be large or small. Perhaps our aim is to raise awareness for a social cause, increase sales, alter the way people view the arts or politics, improve the way our child eats, sway people's perception of ourselves, improve people's understanding of how the world works, increase our team's productivity, or maybe just convince our spouse to work less and join us on a tropical vacation.

Here is the problem, though: we approach this task from inside our own heads. When attempting to create impact, we first and foremost consider ourselves. We reflect on what is persuasive to us, our state of mind, our desires, and our goals. But, of course, if we want to affect the behaviors and beliefs of the person in front of us, we need to first understand what goes on inside *their* head and go along with how *their* brain works.

Take Dr. Carson, for example. As a trained physician and scientist, he was convinced by data showing that vaccines do not cause autism. He therefore assumed that said data would persuade everyone else. Humans, however, are not wired to react dispassionately to information. Numbers and statistics are necessary and wonderful for uncovering the truth, but they're not enough to change beliefs, and they are practically useless for motivating action. This is true whether you are trying to change one mind or many—a whole room of potential investors or just your spouse. Consider climate change: there are mountains of data indicating that humans play a role in warming the globe, yet 50 percent of the population does not believe it.[3] Consider politics: no number will convince a hard-core Republican that a Democratic president has advanced the nation, and vice versa. What about health? Hundreds of studies demonstrate that exercise is good for you and people believe this to be so, yet this knowledge fails miserably at getting many to step on a treadmill.

In fact, the tsunami of information we are receiving today can make us even less sensitive to data because we've become accustomed to finding support for absolutely anything we want to believe, with a simple click of the mouse. Instead, our desires are what shape our beliefs. It is those motivations and feelings we need to tap into to make a change, whether within ourselves or in others.

In this book, I will describe our instincts regarding influence—those habits we fall back on when trying to change others' beliefs and behaviors. Many of these instincts—from trying to scare people into action to insisting that the other is wrong or attempting to exert control—are incompatible with how the mind operates. The principal idea of this book is that an attempt to change someone's mind will be successful if it aligns with the core elements that govern how we think. Each chapter will focus on one of seven critical factors—priors (as in prior beliefs), emotion, incentives, agency, curiosity, state of mind, and other people—and will explain how that factor can hinder or help an attempt to influence.

The difference between familiarizing ourselves with these factors and remaining ignorant is that familiarity will enable you to critically evaluate your behavior, whether you are influencing or being influenced. The majority of the time, I will take on the point of view of the person aiming to influence, but every so often I will flip the relationship and look at things from the perspective of the person being influenced. What goes on in your brain when you listen to another person's opinion? Of course, if you understand one side of the coin, you will better understand the other, too.

We still have a lot of research to conduct to fully understand the factors that influence our minds, but the partial knowledge we already have is tremendously valuable. For example, understanding how the brain's reward system is connected to the motor system reveals when people are more likely to be influenced by carrots and when by sticks. Knowing how stress affects the brain explains why people hugely overreact to negative news following terrorist attacks.

Throughout the book we will shift back and forth from the

corridors of your brain, where neurons are constantly communicating with one another, to the corridors of my lab, where I record people's behavioral and physiological reactions. We'll also tour the world outside: a hospital on the East Coast of the United States that went from failing terribly at getting its medical staff to sanitize their hands to reaching nearly 90 percent compliance in one day, a nursing home in Connecticut where the residents' health was improved by increasing their sense of control, a teenage girl who unknowingly induced psychosomatic symptoms in thousands, and more. My question will always be *why?* Why did this strategy cause a reaction but another did not? Why do we respond to John but ignore Jake? If you know what causes people to react the way they do, you will have the tools to solve the specific challenges you encounter in your own life every day.

1

⟨⟨⟩⟩

Does Evidence Change Beliefs? (Priors)

*The Power of Confirmation and
the Weakness of Data*

Thelma and Jeremiah are happily married. They see eye to eye on most issues; they agree on how to raise their kids and how to handle their finances; they have the same beliefs with regard to politics and religion, similar humor and cultural preferences, and even share the same occupation—both are attorneys. This is not surprising. Research has shown again and again that the best predictor for a long-lasting marriage is not passion or friendship; it is similarity. Opposites, contrary to popular belief, neither attract nor remain an item when they do.[1]

There is, however, one topic Thelma and Jeremiah disagree on. This is not startling, either. Most couples, as compatible as they may be, will argue for years over one issue or another. Maybe it is whether they should have kids, how many to have, how to achieve a work-life balance, or whether to adopt a pet lizard or a guinea pig. For Thelma and Jeremiah, the conflict is over where to settle down. Thelma was born and raised in France, Jeremiah in the United States. Both believe their native country is the best place to raise a family.

Thelma and Jeremiah are not alone. Surveys show that when asked for the ideal place to live, work, raise children, and retire, most people say it is their home country. Only 13 percent of the world's adults would like to leave their country permanently.[2] The grass, it appears, is greenest exactly where you are. If people must immigrate, they prefer to move next door: the French to the United Kingdom, Austrians to Switzerland.

Unfortunately, the solution to Thelma and Jeremiah's problem cannot lie in meeting the other person halfway. Just as having half a kid is not an answer for couples who disagree on whether to expand their unit, Thelma and Jeremiah are unable to build a home in the Atlantic Ocean, midway between Europe and North America. The only solution, then, is for one to convince the other that *their* view is correct.

You would think that Thelma and Jeremiah are perfectly suited for the task. As I mentioned, they are both attorneys. Their life's work is to persuade a jury to take their side. They have set out to solve their marital problem as they would a professional legal problem—each presents the other side with facts and figures to support their argument in an attempt to smash the opposition. Jeremiah shows Thelma data suggesting that the cost of living is lower in the United States, while Thelma provides Jeremiah with numbers proving that attorneys make more money in France. Jeremiah e-mails Thelma an article arguing that the education system is superior in the States, while Thelma finds a different piece claiming that kids are happier in France. Both regard the "evidence" provided by the other as unreliable and refuse to budge. Over the years, they each become more and more grounded in their belief.

The approach taken by Thelma and Jeremiah is one that many of us adopt. Our instinct, when arguing or debating, is to burst in with ammunition that reveals why we are right and the other side is wrong. We articulately present our logical arguments and support them with facts, because these sound very convincing to us. Yet think about the last time you argued with your spouse or participated in a dinner party that transformed into a late-night political debate. Did you manage to nudge people's beliefs? Did they take note of your well-thought-out arguments and carefully researched data? If your recollections are genuine, you probably recognize that, alas, facts and logic are not the most powerful tools for altering opinions. When it comes to arguing, our instincts are wrong.

The Weakness of Data

Your brain, like most people's, is programmed to get a kick out of information. This makes our current digital era an explosive celebration for your mind. While the agricultural age gave us easier access to nutrition, and the industrial age dramatically increased our quality of life, no other era provided as much stimulation for our brains as the information age. It is as if, finally, the human brain has succeeded in building its own amusement park, complete with thrill rides, which are perfectly customized . . . for itself.

Consider the numbers: there are 3 billion Internet users worldwide; every day we produce approximately 2.5 billion gigabytes of data, perform 4 billion Google searches, and watch 10 billion YouTube videos. In the short time it took you to read the last sentence, approximately 530,243 new Google searches were executed and 1,184,390 YouTube videos played around the globe.[3]

It would seem that the digital revolution should come in handy when we are trying to alter people's beliefs. If people love information, what better way to influence their beliefs and actions than to offer data? With big data at our fingertips and powerful computers at our disposal, we can run analyses to expand our knowledge and then share the resulting facts and figures. Seems straightforward, right?

That is, until you attempt to present your carefully collected data and thoughtfully constructed conclusions to the person you are hoping to influence. At that moment, you quickly realize that data is often not the answer when it comes to changing minds.

This epiphany came as a terrible blow to the scientist in me. As a cognitive neuroscientist, I work at the intersection between psychology and neuroscience. Like most scientists, I love data. Some people collect precious rocks; others collect first-edition books, stamps, shoes, vintage cars, or china dolls. I collect data. My computers hold hundreds of folders with thousands of files, each containing rows and rows of numbers. Every number represents an observation: a person's response to a decision problem or their reaction to another human; other numbers indicate the activity in a person's brain or the density of their neuronal fibers. Numbers on their own are useless. The reason I love data is that those rows and rows of numbers can be transformed into something beautiful: meaningful graphs, which, every so often, reveal an exciting new insight into what makes you and me, *Homo sapiens*, tick.

So you can imagine my dismay when I learned that all those numbers, from numerous experiments and observations, pointed to the fact that people are not in fact driven by facts, or figures, or data. It is not that people are stupid; nor are we ridiculously stubborn. It is that the accessibility to lots of data, analytic tools, and powerful computers is the product of the last few decades, while the brains we are attempting to influence are the product of millions of decades. As it turns out, while we adore data, the currency by which our brains assess said data and make decisions is very different from the currency many of us believe our brains should use. The problem with an approach that prioritizes information and logic is that it ignores the core of what makes you and me human: our motives, our fears, our hopes and desires. As we will see, this presents a serious problem; it means that data has only a limited capacity to alter the strong opinions of others. Established beliefs can be extremely resistant to change, even when scientific evidence is provided to undermine those beliefs.

The Power of Confirmation

Three scientists, Charles Lord, Lee Ross, and Mark Lepper, recruited forty-eight American undergraduates who either strongly supported the death penalty or strongly opposed it.[4] They presented them with two scientific studies; one offered evidence regarding the effectiveness of capital punishment, and the other data showed its ineffectiveness. In reality, the studies had been fabricated. Lord, Ross, and Lepper had made them up, but the students did not know that. Did the students find the studies convincing? Did they believe that the data provided good evidence that should alter their minds? They did!

But only when the study reinforced their original view. Those students who strongly supported capital punishment thought the study that demonstrated its effectiveness was well conducted. At the same time, they argued that the other study was poorly executed and not compelling. Those who were originally against capital punishment assessed the studies the other way around. As a result, believers in the death penalty left the lab supporting capital punishment with more passion than ever, while those in opposition to it ended up opposing capital punishment with more zest than before. Rather than enabling people to see both sides of the coin, the exercise polarized everyone involved.

Information can lead to polarization of opinions in domains ranging from abortion and homosexuality to the assassination of John F. Kennedy.[5] My colleague Cass Sunstein (the administrator of the White House Office of Information and Regulatory Affairs during the Obama administration and a current Harvard Law professor) and I wanted to know whether the same was true for beliefs about climate change.[6] We first asked a group of volunteers about their opinions regarding climate change. (For example: Did they believe that man-made climate change was occurring? Did they support the Paris agreement to reduce greenhouse gas emissions?) Based on their answers, we divided them into weak believers in man-made climate change and strong believers. We then informed everyone that climate scientists estimated that the average global temperature would rise by approximately six degrees Fahrenheit by 2100, and asked them for their own estimates of the likely temperature rise by 2100.

Then came the real test. Half of the volunteers were told that in recent weeks prominent scientists had reassessed the data and concluded that the situation was far better than previously thought, suggesting a likely temperature increase of only one to five degrees. Half were told that in recent weeks, prominent scientists had reassessed the data and concluded that the situation was far worse than previously thought, suggesting a likely temperature increase of seven to eleven degrees. All the participants were then asked to provide a new personal estimate.

Did people change their estimates in light of the experts' assessments? Once again, we observed that people altered their opinions only if they'd received information that fit their original worldview. The weak believers in man-made climate change were influenced by the comforting news that the situation was better than previously thought (their estimate dropped by about one degree), but the alarming news had no impact whatsoever on their new estimates. Strong believers showed the exact opposite pattern— they were moved by learning that scientists now thought the situation was even worse than previously believed, but were less influenced by the news that scientists now thought the problem was not as dire.

When you provide someone with new data, they quickly accept evidence that confirms their preconceived notions (what are known as *prior* beliefs) and assess counterevidence with a critical eye. Because we are often exposed to contradicting information and opinions, this tendency will generate polarization, which will expand with time as people receive more and more information.[7]

In fact, presenting people with information that contradicts their opinion can cause them to come up with altogether new counterarguments that further strengthen their original view; this is known as the "boomerang effect." Thelma, for example, found many faults in the article Jeremiah sent her that argued that the education system was better in the United States. "The article was written by an American," she thought to herself, "what do they know about education, anyway? Americans teach 'modern' literature and 'new' history while ignoring ancient writings and Old World narratives."

Did you notice what Thelma did? Not only did she discard any unwelcome evidence, but she came up with new reasons for why the education system was better in France—arguments she had never considered before. As a result, she grew more confident in her initial conviction. Being confronted with evidence that seemed to oppose her strong views made Thelma feel uncomfortable, and so she resolved this negative feeling by rationalizing away the contradicting opinion and reinforcing her own. This is why by marrying Jeremiah, Thelma became a stronger advocate for France. If she had married her old high school sweetheart François, I suspect she would have had a less idealistic view of her home country.

Google Is (Always) on My Side

There is no single truth we all agree on. In a letter to Jean-Baptiste LeRoy in 1789, Benjamin Franklin famously wrote, "In this world nothing can be said to be certain, except death and taxes." Franklin borrowed this phrase from the English writer Daniel Defoe, who in his 1726 book *The Political History of the Devil* said, "Things as certain as death and taxes, can be more firmly believ'd."[8] While the "death and taxes" expression is commonly used, neither of these things are in fact truths we all conform to. Some believe death can be overcome, perhaps by cryonics or engineering. Even if we acknowledge the end is certain, there are many diverse views on what lies on the other side. And there are certainly a number of tax evaders and "tax protestors," people who dismiss the idea that taxes are a necessity. If we do not all agree on the certainty of death and taxes, you can imagine we are bound to disagree on a large number of other "truths."

Whether living in France is better than living in the United States is a matter of opinion. Whether capital punishment is morally right is also a subjective question. What happens when a disagreement involves hard facts? For example, consider the question of where Barack Obama was born. The controversy over Obama's birthplace started in 2008 when anonymous e-mails were released that questioned whether he was in fact a natural-born citizen.[9] If Obama had not been born in the United States, he would not have been eligible to run for president. "Evidence" supporting these allegations soon appeared on the Internet. The issue created such a media firestorm that Obama decided to address the question directly and supply his birth certificate. Yet a validated certificate from a U.S. president was not enough to change people's opinions. Surveys showed that a non-negligible percentage of Americans were still not sure that Barack Obama was eligible to serve as president.[10]

"There is a mechanism, a network of misinformation that in a new media era can get churned out there constantly," Obama noted in 2010. This was his response to the revelation that two years after the presidential election, 20 percent of Americans (fully one-fifth!) still did not believe he had been born in the United States.[11] By "mechanism" and "network," Obama was most likely referring to the technology boosting the spread of misinformation.

In today's world, the ease by which we can find "data" and "evidence" to discredit any opinion—and, at the same time, uncover new information to support our own—is unprecedented. It takes less than a second to turn up articles suggesting that strawberries are bad for you (it seems their thin skin allows unwanted chemicals in) and butter in your coffee is good for you. The latter trend is known as "Bulletproof Coffee." Apparently, Bulletproof Coffee "has a massive impact on cognitive function" and "will keep you satisfied with level energy for six hours if you need it . . . programming your body to burn fat for energy all day long."[12] It takes another second to find just as many articles suggesting that strawberries are in fact good for you, because of their great nutrients, and butter in coffee is a very bad idea. It seems that saturated fat is good, but humans did not evolve eating such massive amounts of it. As a result, there have been reports of dramatically elevated cholesterol levels due to Bulletproof Coffee.[13]

Paradoxically then, the wealth of available information makes us more resistant to change, because it is so easy to find data that support our own vision. This is true even for extreme views, such as believing that your own race is genetically superior to others. We carefully read blogs and articles that support our opinions, and we may avoid clicking on links that offer a different take.

This is only half the problem, though. What we are not aware of is that cherry-picking information is done for us under the radar. We are oblivious to the fact that often we are presented with filtered information to suit our preestablished beliefs. This is how it works: when you enter a search term into Google or another search engine, you get results that have been customized for you, according to your past searches and Web activity.[14] In other words, if you are a Democrat searching for the latest stats on the presidential debate, your search will most likely spit back news articles and blogs from Democrats who think the Democratic candidate did superbly. The links will include news websites and opinion blogs you have visited previously and others associated with them. Given that the first twenty results you get all praise the performance of the Democratic candidate, you are left with the impression that, indeed, she or he delivered an outstanding performance. Everyone thinks so. In fact, your Twitter and Facebook feeds provide further evidence of the superiority of your candidate, making you more and more confident of the upcoming election result.

Here is the thing, though: if you are a Republican, your feed will be quite different. This is because your Twitter and Facebook accounts will likely be associated with the accounts of other Republicans. Your Google search will also provide you with different results. This is not only because Google uses sophisticated algorithms to learn about your specific interests and preferences but also because searches take into account your geographical location.[15] Google wants to give you exactly what you are looking for.

It assumes that what you are looking for is similar to what your neighbor Riana is interested in and different from what Pinto is searching for across the globe in Uganda. That is a reasonable assumption. So you end up with links to websites frequently viewed by users in your area. Now, because Republicans are more likely to live in certain states and Democrats in other states, your search for "presidential debate" spits back links to websites supporting your candidate (assuming you are living in a state where the majority resides with your preferred political party). Since this happens under the radar, you become more and more confident in your political views, as well as your cultural preferences and scientific beliefs.

This process can make us weaker. How can we reasonably decide what is true and what is right if we are not even exposed to other streams of thought? There are actions you can take to minimize this technology-induced confirmation bias. Here is a tip: if you want to minimize Internet searches that are customized to your beliefs, use "anonymous browsing" or delete the information your search browser holds on you (such as location) and disable history tracking. You may also decide to update the accounts you follow on social media to include unusual suspects—people whom you respect but who advocate for positions you disagree with. Perhaps those people will follow you in return.

There is another artificial way by which our views can be confirmed without us realizing it. It is the "social-feedback loop." Imagine that you've found a wonderful new product and you want to share your exciting discovery with all your friends, so they, too, can benefit. Let's say the product is a new wireless router known as the "super router." It enables very fast connections over large distances. You tell your friends and relatives about it and post it on Pinterest, Instagram, and other social networks. Over the next couple of months, something intriguing happens. You keep hearing about the "super router" from acquaintances, both in person and online. "Have you heard about this super-powerful new wireless router?" they ask. "Supposedly it can change the way you surf the Web." These are not even people in your immediate circle—it seems that everyone now knows about the "super router." What you may be underestimating, though, is how much of this buzz was triggered by you. When we share an idea, recommendation, or opinion with a large number of people, some of them will share the information with others, who may share it with still others. Because social networks tend to be heavily intertwined, eventually those opinions will loop back to you, only you may not realize that you were the source. Instead, you may conclude that many other people have independently formed the exact same opinion, further strengthening your view.

Using Your Intelligence to Twist Information

Seeking out and interpreting data in a way that strengthens our preestablished opinions is known as the "confirmation bias."[16] It is one of the strongest biases humans hold. Now that you are acutely aware of it, you will probably observe people engaging in this type of thinking every day; you may catch them disregarding arguments that do not suit them and embracing those that do. You will also notice, however, that individuals differ in this tendency; some are more resistant than others. What makes some people take in information in a balanced manner while others discount evidence that does not fit their existing opinions?

If you perceive yourself as highly analytic—someone who has a strong ability to make use of quantitative data and a good reasoning capacity—embrace yourself. People with stronger analytic abilities are more likely to twist data at will than people with low reasoning ability.[17] In one study 1,111 Americans from across the country participated in an online task. First they were given a battery of standard tests to measure their quantitative abilities and use of systematic logic. Then they were given one of two data sets. They were led to believe that the first was from a study examining a new skin-rash treatment. The participants were asked to figure out from the data if the skin-rash treatment was helping the patients' condition or making it worse. To solve this problem, they needed to use their quantitative skills. It comes as no surprise that people who had earlier scored higher on the mathematical tests also did better at analyzing the skin-rash-treatment data.

The second set of data showed crime statistics in different cities. The volunteers were told that "a city government was trying to decide whether to pass a law banning private citizens from carrying concealed handguns in public. Government officials were unsure whether the law will be more likely to decrease crime by reducing the number of people carrying weapons or increase crime by making it harder for law-abiding citizens to defend themselves from violent criminals. To address this question, researchers had divided cities into two groups: one consisting of cities that had recently enacted bans on concealed weapons and another that had no such bans."

The volunteers had to examine the data and conclude whether the new law was causing crime to increase or decrease.

In reality, the skin-rash-treatment data set and the gun-control data set were exactly the same. The same set of numbers was used. Yet the participants did better at solving the problem when the numbers were presented as data from a new skin-rash-treatment study than a gun-control-"treatment" study. Why?

The participants did not care if the new skin treatment was

working or not, so they addressed the task rationally, using their math abilities in the service of carefully analyzing the data. However, most participants had passionate opinions on gun control, and this passion interfered with their ability to analyze the data objectively. So far, nothing new—we know that motivation taints our ability to reason. Here is the fascinating part, though: those people who were good with numbers—the "analytic" ones—were the worst at accurately assessing whether a gun-control ban reduced crime.

These findings debunk the idea that motivated reasoning is somewhat a trait of less intelligent people. To the contrary, the greater your cognitive capacity, the greater your ability to rationalize and interpret information at will, and to creatively twist data to fit your opinions. Ironically, then, people may use their intelligence not to draw more accurate conclusions but to find fault in data they are unhappy with. This is why, when arguing with others, our instinct for offering facts and figures that support our view and contradict theirs may not be the optimal approach. Even if the person in front of you is highly intelligent, you may find it difficult to change their mind with counterevidence.

Why We Are the Way We Are

This raises the question: why have we evolved a brain that discards perfectly valid information when that information does not fit with its current view of the world? This may seem like bad engineering, potentially leading to many errors in judgment. So why hasn't this glitch been corrected for over the course of human evolution? Could it be that there is a reasonable explanation for our apparent folly? A benefit, perhaps?

Some scholars ascertain that the human brain evolved the ability to reason not in order to uncover the truth but to enable us to persuade others that we are right.[18] The idea is that you evaluate the evidence in front of you in a way that will help you argue your views more effectively. If we are better at arguing, the story goes, we will be more likely to get our way. This theory can account for the confirmation bias and the boomerang effect. I find it somewhat unconvincing, though. The idea that the human brain evolved to be able to reason purely so that we can win an argument seems weak. What's more, if most of us possess a confirmation bias, then none of us will be able to persuade the others anyway. In fact, the most influential individuals are often the most open-minded.

Let's explore another possibility—the idea that interpreting information in light of what we already think we know is often the correct approach. *On average*, when you encounter a piece of data that contradicts what you already know about the world, that piece of data is, in fact, wrong. For example, if someone claims they observed a yellow elephant flying in the sky or a purple fish walking on the ground, it is reasonable to assume that this person is lying or delusional. We should, generally speaking, evaluate information in relation to what we already know.

Four factors come into play when we form a new belief: our old belief (this is technically known as the "prior"), our confidence in that old belief, the new evidence, and our confidence in that evidence. For example, imagine that an adult is told by their young child that there is an elephant flying in the sky. The parent holds a strong belief that elephants cannot fly. In addition, they do not have strong confidence in their child's credibility, so they will conclude the child is wrong. Now imagine the reverse: a very young child is told by their parent that an elephant is flying in the sky. The child has not yet formed strong beliefs regarding the world, so they are not certain whether elephants can fly or not. Moreover, they hold their parents' opinions in high regard, so they conclude that elephants can fly.

On balance, this approach to changing our beliefs is a reasonable one. In many cases we *should* indeed hold on to what we know. However, a side effect of this process is that preestablished opinions are very difficult to change, even when they are wrong.

How Much Is It Costing Us?

We have already seen that people's tendency to disregard evidence that does not fit their views interferes with their personal relationships, and also with politics. This is alarming in and of itself. What about finance? Are people selectively interpreting information when making financial decisions? My colleagues Andreas Kappes and Read Montague and I conducted an experiment to find out.[19]

Millie was one of the many participants in our study. She was a twenty-year-old undergraduate at University College London majoring in biology. She had straight brown hair, which she kept in a ponytail, and large seventies-style spectacles that framed twinkly eyes. Like most students, she needed some extra cash to pay her rent, and so when she stumbled upon our ad for a paid study on the Psychology Department website, she was quick to sign up. When Millie arrived at our lab, she was introduced to her partner in crime, Ewan, who was also participating in our study. She had never met Ewan before. From a brief introduction, Millie learned that Ewan was a psychology major who had just returned from a semester abroad in Japan.

Andreas, the experimenter, explained to Millie and Ewan that they were about to play a game that involved real estate assessment. The better they performed on the task, the more money they would earn. Both Millie's and Ewan's knowledge of real estate boiled down to their experiences renting a room in an apartment in London. Yet they were determined to do the best they could on the task.

Andreas told Millie and Ewan that they would be escorted to separate rooms; each would work on a computer and be presented with a couple hundred different real estate properties. For each property, they would be shown information similar to what you would find on a real estate website: a photo of the real estate, information regarding its location, size, and so on. They would then need to indicate if they believed the property was worth more or less than a million dollars, and how much they were willing to bet that they were correct.

For example, a West Hollywood three-bedroom home, 3,959 square feet with a pool—on sale for more or less than $1 million? Millie thinks it's more and is willing to bet £2 she is right. If she is correct, she will win £2; if she is wrong, she will lose £2. After Millie enters her bet, she has an opportunity to learn of Ewan's bet. In this case, it turns out that Ewan disagrees. He believes the home is worth less than $1 million and is willing to bet £3 on it.

According to the rules of the game, Millie cannot change her vote, but she can change the amount of money riding on it. If she thinks Ewan is right, she can withdraw her bet altogether; that way she will neither lose nor win. Or she can lower her bet to a pound or less. She also has the opportunity to increase her bet if she wants to.

Like most of our participants, Millie does nothing. When Ewan disagrees with her, she ignores him. On the surface, that seems reasonable. Why should Millie listen to Ewan anyway? He is a psychology major, not a real estate agent. Most likely, he does not know more than she does. Millie's decision seems sensible. Except for one thing: when Ewan *agrees* with her, she ups her bet. In other words, when Ewan makes the same judgment as Millie, his opinion is deemed sufficiently trustworthy to warrant a larger investment. Yet when he takes another view, his opinion is deemed useless.

Millie is not a rare case. On average, participants in our study significantly increased their bet after learning that their partner *agreed* with their real estate judgment but in most cases did nothing when that exact same partner, with the exact same credentials, *disagreed* with the judgment. The mind seems to happily adopt opinions most convenient to its established views.

This study illustrates an important point. On the one hand, it is well known that people are extremely susceptible to social influence; we follow trends, we mimic others, and we often do so subconsciously. (Later in the book, I will expand on our strong tendency for social learning.) On the other hand, once people have committed to a decision or opinion, it is difficult for one person to persuade them to adopt a new one. In the face of prior decisions and beliefs, social influence may fail.

Andreas's findings seem to contradict a classic assumption in economics—namely, that investors are able to learn from new information (such as the opinions of others) irrespective of their past financial decisions. We now know that this assumption is false. People put more weight on information that supports their previous investments and less weight on information that undermines them.

Take, for example, research conducted by Camelia Kuhnen, a neuroeconomist at the University of North Carolina, and her colleagues.[20] Kuhnen asked approximately fifty people to make a series of one hundred investment decisions between a risky stock and a safe bond with known payoffs. After each choice, the current stock's dividends were revealed and another choice was offered. Kuhnen and her colleagues found that if people selected the stock and observed a high dividend, they were likely to think the stock was good. However, if they selected the stock and, to their disappointment, observed a low dividend, they ignored the data altogether rather than assume the stock was bad.

Just as Millie's real estate decisions interfered with her ability to listen to Ewan's advice when he disagreed with her, prior investments interfere with people's ability to alter their financial expectations when new data does not fit with their past choices. Across domains, people discount information that goes against their previous decisions—and this can come with a financial cost.

Kuhnen and her colleagues did more than just observe behavior; they also recorded people's brain activity to try to understand what exactly was going on inside their heads. They found that when participants received information that did not fit with their prior decisions, their brains—metaphorically speaking—"shut off."* For example, when a participant selected a stock and then observed that it gave a low dividend, their brain responses were reduced. In contrast, when new data confirmed a person's past choices, enhanced activation was observed in a large network of regions. Andreas and I noticed a similar pattern in our study; a person's brain was very sensitive to information following the revelation that someone had made similar choices, less so following the revelation that someone had made dissimilar choices.

These results may seem surprising, because many times when people discover that they may be wrong, a large reaction—known as an "error signal"—is observed in the brain. However, what this study tells us is that in those cases in which we have already committed to a belief or action, we may ignore evidence suggesting that we might be wrong. We interpret such data as unreliable; if

---

* I emphasize that this is a metaphor; the brain does not literally "shut off."

the new evidence is invalid in our eyes, then we might not bother to pay close attention to it.

What then, if anything, can we do to change beliefs? Surely opinions do not always remain stable—they *do* evolve. So how can we create change?

Altering the Old or Building Anew?

Imagine the following scenario: you are a pediatrician in the midst of a busy day at the clinic. Your two p.m. appointment enters your office with his toddler for a checkup. After completing the physical examination and inquiring about the child's motor, language, and social development, you address the topic of the child's vaccines. The child's father, however, is deeply concerned about the MMR (measles, mumps, and rubella) vaccine. He has heard that it increases the risk of autism.

The number of parents refusing to vaccinate their children has risen since a now infamous 1998 study first suggested a link between the vaccine and autism.[21] The study was published by Dr. Andrew Wakefield and his team; at the time, Wakefield was an honorary consultant at the Royal Free Hospital School of Medicine in London. Wakefield's basic claim was that when measles, mumps, and rubella vaccines were given at the same time, they modified the immune system of the child. This enabled the measles virus to penetrate the intestines and for certain proteins to escape from the intestines and reach the brain. Those proteins could then damage neurons, causing autism.[22] Although the article was published in the prestigious journal the *Lancet*, it was later discredited. Research conducted in subsequent years concluded that there was no connection between the MMR vaccine and autism.[23]

Yet the flame ignited by Wakefield's research failed to go out. In the face of abundant scientific evidence to the contrary, many people still fear the risk of the MMR vaccine's alleged side effects and refuse to let their children be vaccinated. As a result, the number of measles cases is on the rise. In 2014, there were 644 cases reported in the United States, which is a threefold increase relative to 2013.

Back at the clinic, you, the doctor, are faced with the difficult task of persuading the parent in front of you to vaccinate his child. What approach should you take? Most people's instinct is to inform the parent of scientific evidence showing that the MMR vaccine does not cause autism. Undermining vaccination myths is also the approach adopted by the Centers for Disease Control and Prevention. This seems a reasonable tactic. Yet studies show that it does not work. This is because information is evaluated relative to preestablished beliefs. The further away new data is from one's established beliefs, the less likely it is to be considered valid. In fact, by repeating the myths regarding the MMR vaccine in an attempt to dispel them, people sometimes wind up remembering the myths rather than the counterevidence.

To solve this problem, a group of psychologists from UCLA and the University of Illinois at Urbana-Champaign came up with a new idea. Instead of dispelling a cemented belief, they would attempt to implant a new one altogether.[24] Their reasoning was that a parent's decision about whether to vaccinate their child is determined by two factors: the negative side effects of the vaccine and the positive results of being vaccinated. Parents who refuse to vaccinate their child already hold strong beliefs regarding the possible side effect—the alleged increased risk of autism. Trying to alter this perception results in resistance. Instead of attempting to persuade people that the MMR vaccine does not cause autism, the researchers would highlight the fact that the MMR vaccine prevents the likelihood of potentially deadly illnesses. This is the path of least resistance—people have no reason to doubt that the vaccine will protect their child from measles, mumps, and rubella. The team's approach involved finding some common ground: both the parents' and the doctors' priority was the health of the child. Focusing on what they had in common, rather than what they disagreed about, enabled change.

The solution was found to be effective. Highlighting the ability of

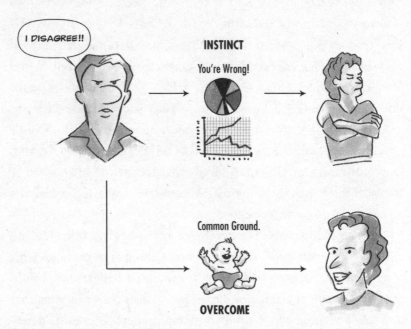

Figure 1.1. Priors. *Influence behavior by building on common ground instead of trying to prove others wrong. Our instinct is to try to alter people's beliefs and actions by introducing data to prove that we are right and they are wrong. It often fails, because in the face of facts that clash with their prior beliefs, people tend to come up with counterarguments or turn away. Instead, find arguments that rely on common ground. For example, telling parents who refuse to vaccinate their children that science has shown that vaccines do not cause autism did not alter the parents' behavior. Instead, saying that vaccines would protect their children from deadly diseases was more effective—the argument did not contradict their prior beliefs and was compatible with the common goal of keeping children healthy.*

the MMR vaccine to protect children from devastating illness was more likely to change people's intentions about vaccinations than attempting to dispel fears of its side effects. When an established belief is difficult to weed out, seeding a new one may be the answer.

* * *

Let's return to Thelma and Jeremiah. Remember them? They were the married attorneys who disagreed on where in the world they should settle down. Jeremiah was trying to convince Thelma that the United States was more desirable than France, and Thelma was saying, *"Non! La France est mieux."* They were both trying to find reasonable arguments for why one place was better than the other—baguette against white bread, the Louvre versus the Metropolitan Museum of Art—but they were getting nowhere. Thelma was disregarding Jeremiah's arguments, and he was ignoring hers. The problem was that to accept the other's case, they each had to let go of their own beliefs.

What would happen, though, if Thelma presented Jeremiah with an argument that did not conflict with his existing views? For example, she could say—"the U.S. is indeed a wonderful place to work and raise kids, but I will be happier being close to my parents." Or she could show Jeremiah data that is already close to his heart—perhaps a study arguing that the top two countries in which to raise a family are France and the United States. Such data would fit Jeremiah's preexisting beliefs, so he would pay attention. The new information could provide an initial shift toward her view. In contrast, if she were to claim that the United States is one of the worst countries in which to settle down, Jeremiah would just turn away.

Whether it is a debate about gun control, football, vaccinations, or a domestic disagreement, to shift opinions we need to first consider the other person's mind. What are their preestablished notions? What are their motivations? When we have a strong motivation to believe that something is true, even the sturdiest of proof to the contrary will fall on deaf ears. Thelma wanted to move back to France, so she was highly motivated to find any article, blog, or figure that showed her country's superiority. Those supporting capital punishment were motivated to believe data showing its effectiveness and to find fault with statistics showing otherwise. Those who opposed Obama had a strong motivation to believe that he had not been born in America.

Beliefs rarely stand on their own; they are intertwined with a network of other beliefs and drives. Considering the other person's existing outlook will help clarify how we can present arguments in a way most convincing to them, rather than a way most convincing to us. While we may instinctively launch into an argument with a hefty sack of evidence to explain why we are right and the other side is wrong, this may lead us astray. What the studies described in this chapter teach us is that the person on the other side will likely shut down or fiercely find counterarguments. To successfully elicit change, we therefore need to identify common motivations. As we will see in the next chapter, once we identify those common goals, we then need to call upon our emotions to help get the message across.

⎯⎯⧁⧂⧀⎯⎯

2

How We Were Persuaded to Reach
for the Moon
(Emotion)

The Incredible Sway of Emotion

On a hot September day in 1962, President John F. Kennedy was standing in the Rice University football stadium. He was in Texas to persuade the crowd of thirty-five thousand in front of him, as well as the rest of the nation, to support a risky project that would cost the country almost $6 billion and could well end up being a complete failure. The plan was to reach the moon.[1] Literally.

If you were born after July 21, 1969, you may find it difficult to conceive of a reality in which Neil Armstrong had not set foot on the Earth's only natural satellite. Yet if you were around in the early 1960s, you may recall that the decision to transport a living human being to the moon and back was far from obvious.

Kennedy himself had not always been convinced of the need to conquer the moon. A year earlier, he had rejected a budget request from NASA that was aimed at sending a man to the moon within the decade. His attitude, however, changed when it became apparent that the Soviets were beating the Americans at the space game 2–0. Not only were they the first to launch an artificial satellite—*Sputnik*—but they were also the first to send a man—Yuri Gagarin—into space. The Americans had a lot of catching up to do. The first U.S. attempt to launch a satellite was nicknamed project "Flopnik," for the satellite exploded a few seconds after liftoff, on live TV no less. Sending the first American—Alan Shepard—into space was more successful. However, his trip took place three weeks after Gagarin's launch, and unlike Gagarin, Shepard did not orbit the Earth. All of this resulted in domestic humiliation and fear of a Soviet-ruled outer space.[2]

The president felt it was crucial that the Americans win the next round and decided that the U.S. government should set its sights on the moon. The fact that neither the Americans nor the Soviets had the technology needed to land a man on the moon was actually an advantage. It meant the Americans might have time to catch up with the USSR.

His first step was to convince the citizens of the urgent need to go to the moon. The support of many was essential not only because a significant percentage of U.S. taxpayers' money would be allocated to fulfill the dream, but also because the collaboration of thousands of scientists, engineers, technicians, and other professionals across the country would be required to achieve this goal. Kennedy had to rally popular support for the program, and he was at Rice's football stadium to do just that. He stepped up to the podium, and for the next seventeen minutes and forty seconds, he explained to the American people why he believed that approximately 4 percent of that year's budget should be spent on the "greatest adventure on which man has ever embarked."[3]

The impact was tremendous. When he was done, every lion, giraffe, and penguin in Houston's nearby zoo could hear the crowd cheering. The speech made headlines across the country and greatly enhanced NASA's profile. Some have speculated that were it not for that speech, as well as a similar one JFK had made to Congress shortly beforehand, we might still be reaching for the moon.[4]

We often take it for granted that one person can have such a tremendous impact on so many. One idea, delivered in the form of a speech, a song, or a story, can change the minds and actions of millions. But if we stop to think about it, this is quite an extraordinary ability humans have—to transmit ideas from one mind to another.

Inside the Mind of the Audience

Think about the last time you spoke in front of a group. Maybe it was a lecture, a presentation at work, or one of those embarrassing wedding toasts. All eyes were on you. Did you ever wonder what was going on inside the minds of those in front of you? I find it intriguing to survey people's expressions and actions while I talk. From the stage, you can see everything. The guy in the corner tweeting, a woman in the front row with her mouth open, another at the back feverishly taking notes. But every so often, the crowd will become a unified entity—gasping together, laughing together, applauding together—in sync. If you are part of such an audience yourself, you can feel the shared response in your body.

In March 2012, I was seated in such a crowd. I was at the Terrace Theater in Long Beach, California, to give a talk at TED's annual conference. My presentation was scheduled for the last day of the conference, and so I spent the week listening to the lectures of the other speakers.

Susan Cain, the author of the book *Quiet*, was on stage at the time. The attendees were uniformly transfixed. At that very moment in Long Beach, it was crystal-clear that her speech would have a broad influence. Indeed, at the time of this writing, Cain's talk has been viewed online more than thirteen million times, and her message about the power of introverts has spread widely.[5] The audience was not aware of it, but the feeling that afternoon in the auditorium in California was related to an intriguing physiological phenomenon, one that predicted her success.

I did not record the firing of neurons in the brains of the thirteen hundred people seated with me in the Terrace Theater listening to Cain, nor of the thirty-five thousand people seated in Rice Stadium listening to JFK. It was not possible then, and it is not possible now. Yet I can make an educated guess as to what we would have observed had we done so.

At Princeton University, a group of researchers recorded the pattern of brain activity, using an MRI scanner, of individuals while they tuned into speeches of politicians.[6] What they found was that while people were listening to powerful speeches, their brains "ticked together." The brain activity of different individuals went up and down in unison, bursting and quieting at the same time, at the same position in the brain, as if they were synchronized.

This observation may seem unsurprising. By definition, an engaging speech captures people's attention. If everyone is listening intently to the same monologue, the audience's brain patterns will look similar. If the speech is as boring as watching paint dry, each mind will drift away to its own wonderland, and the synchronization will be broken. But that is not the whole story.

Synchronization was observed not only in brain regions important for language and hearing but also in those involved in creating associations, in generating and processing emotions, and in enabling us to place ourselves in the shoes of others and feel empathy. Powerful speeches did more than capture people's attention—a commendable feat in and of itself. Powerful speeches shaped people's reactions in a similar manner regardless of a person's personality and past experiences. In other words, whether it was the brain of a twenty-four-year-old liberal woman who liked reading Shakespeare while eating lemon crepes or that of a thirty-seven-year-old conservative man who enjoyed weight lifting on the beach, these speeches created widespread neural activity such that these two different brains would seem functionally alike when examined in an MRI scanner.

Both JFK and Cain managed to get millions not only to *listen* to what they were saying but to feel the way they did, to take on their point of view, and in so doing, they were able to get the crowd to support their quest. But what elements in their respective addresses would have enabled (the presumed) widespread synchronization?

Emotion, the Conductor

The first attempt to look at when, how, and why brains synchronize took place in 2004 at the Weizmann Institute of Science in Israel, and it involved spaghetti Westerns.[7] The participants in this study were asked to lie in an MRI scanner and watch the classic western film *The Good, the Bad and the Ugly*. Their brain activity was recorded as they followed the actions of Clint Eastwood (the Good), Lee Van Cleef (the Bad), and Eli Wallach (the Ugly).

When the researchers at the Weizmann, led by neuroscientists Uri Hasson and Rafi Malach, looked at the pattern of brain activity of all the participants, they found that the minds of the group were generally in sync. However, at certain moments throughout the movie, neural activity was particularly closely orchestrated across individuals. During those moments, a whopping 30 percent of an individual's brain was ticking together with everyone else's brains, making it difficult to distinguish one brain response from another. Hasson and Malach noted down the exact times when this occurred and then watched the film again to see what exactly was going on during those instances.

They found that at the first point in the film during which people's brains had been reacting similarly, there was a surprising shift in the movie plot. The second moment involved a large explosion. The third and fourth—a gunshot. Then another gunshot, and another explosion. A pattern seemed to emerge before their eyes: the moments in which brains had a strong tendency to "unify" were the emotionally charged moments in the film. In the face of events that cause suspense, surprise, and elation, one person's brain looked a lot like another's. Emotion was "hijacking" a large proportion of people's brains and doing so in a uniform manner.

If you think about it, this makes perfect sense. An emotional reaction is the body's way of saying, "Hey, something really important is going on," and it is crucial that you respond accordingly. So crucial that most of your brain is drafted so that you can process the emotion-evoking event and generate a reaction. When something emotional happens, your amygdala—the region in your brain important for signaling arousal—is activated. The amygdala then sends an "alert signal" to the rest of the brain, immediately changing the ongoing activity. It doesn't matter if you are a short Danish lady or a tall Serbian child—all brains are "preprogrammed" to react in *roughly* similar ways to emotion-eliciting stimuli.

For example, if a stranger were to walk into your room this very moment with a large knife, it would immediately elicit a response from your amygdala. The amygdala would call upon your hippocampus, intensifying your memory of the event. It would also alter activity in regions of your cortex, causing you to automatically focus on the knife at the expense of everything else. The function of your hypothalamus, which is your brain's hormonal center, and your brainstem, the region involved in regulating bodily functions such as breathing, would change too, and you would start sweating.

Now, if you are sitting in a movie theater and "the Bad" is pointing his gun at "the Good," there is no need for you to react. You are safe in the dark theater, as the rifle does not pose a real threat to you or anyone else. But the "emotion center" of your brain is programmed to respond fast, before the situation has been fully processed. Because emotion is such a basic, low-level reaction, a similar response is also triggered in the person sitting to your right and the one to your left. Your minds are captured by the emotional event on the screen. Because you are all experiencing a similar physiological state, you are likely to process the story line in a like manner. Emotion promotes brain synchronization by automatically allocating everyone's attention in the same direction and by generating a similar psychological state, which prompts people to act and view the world in a similar way.[8]

Back in the Texas football stadium, Kennedy could have simply outlined his plan for reaching the moon. At the TED conference, Susan Cain could have plainly given numbers that show that introverts are integral to the progression of our society. But instead, Kennedy spoke of the new dangers and opportunities of space exploration, and Cain humorously shared her experience of being a bookwormish child at a cheerleading-obsessed summer camp. They triggered emotions in their audience, and the response increased the neural synchronization between listeners, enhancing similarities in experience and perception.

The speeches most likely had another important effect: enabling the minds of the listeners to "couple" with Kennedy's and Cain's.

Coupling

There is one question most people love being asked. It doesn't matter that the question has been put to them many times before; most will always reply with eagerness.

The question I am referring to is "How did you meet your spouse?" As long as the person is not in the midst of a throat-cutting, backstabbing divorce, they will share with you, at length, the details of that defining moment. If you listen closely, you will notice people saying they "could feel a connection immediately," they "finished each other's sentences," or they "felt they had met before." People are inclined to attribute this sensation to "magic." Well, either that or an effective algorithm on Match.com. Hasson, however, attributes it to brain coupling. A feeling that you "click" with another person occurs when complete comprehension emerges between two communicating individuals, and, according to Hasson, that is the consequence of synchronization.[9] "Coupling is not a result of understanding. It is the neural basis on which we understand one another," he explains.[10]

Such coupling is by no means exclusive to romantic partners. You may even experience it listening to a stranger while inside a brain-imaging scanner. In one study, the brain activity of Princeton undergraduates was recorded in an MRI machine while they listened to a playback of a young woman, whom I will call Annabelle, telling the story of her high school prom.[11] Annabelle's pattern of brain activity was also recorded while she told the story, so that later her neural activity could be compared with that of the students listening to her.

Annabelle's tale begins: "I know everyone has some crazy prom stories, but, well, just wait. I was a freshman in high school in Miami, Florida, and I'm new to the freshman scene. I'm new to the high school scene, I should say, and it's almost December, so I've been in high school for about three months, and this boy Charles asks me out. He's British, he's a junior, and he's really cute but sort of shy but just, well, it doesn't matter. So I say yes, I'm excited."

With humor and suspense, Annabelle goes on to describe her adventures on land and in water. The story includes young love, rejection, blood, alcohol, and a couple of policemen—all the required elements of a best seller.

One of the volunteers in this study was a young man I will call Ronald. From Ronald's neural firing, it was evident that his brain activity quickly became synchronized with Annabelle's while he was listening to her story. This matching of brain patterns could be seen over a large network of neural areas, not only in regions processing language. Then something intriguing happened. After a while, Ronald's pattern of neural activity began to *precede* that of Annabelle's. The listener's brain was now marching ahead of the speaker's brain, predicting what the storyteller would say next. Ronald's brain seemed to anticipate the next turn of events, and this enabled him to comprehend Annabelle's story even better.

If you had heard Annabelle's tale, you would have noticed that it is rich with emotion. She shares her inner affective world with the listener—her excitement, her anxiety, her fear. Emotion is by no means necessary for synchronization, but it heightens it. By physically sharing Annabelle's emotional state, Ronald is provided with a context that can aid his understanding of Annabelle's goals and behavior. Taking her perspective, he can predict her next action. Lauri Nummenmaa, a Finnish neuroscientist who studies brain synchronization, writes that this may be one of the roles of emotion in neural synchronization—to promote social interaction and understanding, and to therefore enhance our ability to predict each other's actions.[12]

Politicians, artists, and anyone with a message to convey are often advised to use emotion to engage an audience. This is thought of as a way to generate interest—an emotional story or speech may seem more stimulating and grab more attention. We know that movies, novels, and songs that elicit emotion tend to be more popular. But Nummenmaa's research suggests that there is more. Emotion equates the physiological state of the listener with that of the speaker, which makes it more likely that the listener will process incoming information in a similar manner to how the speaker sees it. This is why eliciting emotion can help in communicating your ideas and having others share your point of view, whether you are conversing with just one individual or talking to thousands. In other words, if I feel happy and you feel sad, we are unlikely to interpret the same story in the same way. But if I can first help you feel as happy as I do, perhaps by sharing a joke, you will be more likely to construe my message the way I do. The good news about this tactic is that emotion is extremely contagious.

Sharing the Love

I love watching the Olympics. I have to confess, though, that the primary reason I enjoy watching the games is not the incredible achievements of the athletes. It is not for the opportunity to view the fastest man alive or the longest jump ever executed. My deep attraction to the games stems largely from the raw display of emotion: the pure happiness in the eyes of the woman who just crossed the finish line first, the tears of joy running down the face of the swimmer standing on the podium. Their happiness is contagious. You cannot help but smile when those faces on the screen do. Even the most aloof among us will find their eyes welling in response to the winners' and losers' tears.

One of the strongest ways we impact each other is via emotion. Sharing ideas usually takes time and cognitive effort. Sharing feelings, however, happens instantly and easily. The way you feel quickly, automatically, and often unconsciously affects the way those around you feel, and how they feel influences your own emotions.[13] Your coworkers, family, friends, and even strangers will rapidly pick up on your state by perceiving changes in your facial expression, tone of voice, posture, and language. And while they may not be aware of it, if you are happy, they are more likely to become happy; if you are stressed, they are more likely to become stressed.

Our brains are designed to transmit emotions quickly to one another, because emotions often convey important information about our environment. For example, if I detect your fear, I am more likely to feel fear, too, and as a result scan my surroundings for danger. This may save me, because if you are afraid, there is a good chance that there's something nearby I should be afraid of, too. And if I detect your excitement, I am more likely to become excited, which will cause me to scan my surroundings for rewards. This is a good strategy, because if you are excited, there is a good chance that there's something nearby I should be excited about, too. All of this happens rapidly, before we even have the opportunity to think things over.

The ability to feel the pleasure, pain, and stress of others is one we are seemingly born with. If you are a parent, you were no doubt amazed to discover the extent to which your ups and downs were embodied in your children from day one. Take, for example, a study that was conducted in San Francisco by the psychologist Wendy Mendes and her team.[14] Mendes invited sixty-nine mothers and their one-year-old infants into her lab. Her plan was to induce stress in the mothers and then observe the reactions of their babies. Let's zoom in on two such pairs—Rachel and her baby son Roni, and Susan and her baby daughter Sara.

Shortly after Rachel, Roni, Susan, and Sara arrived at the lab, a researcher from Mendes's team attached sensors to their bodies, in order to measure their cardiovascular responses. These recordings would reflect how stressed the mothers and infants were. At this point, everyone was happy and relaxed. The babies were then taken to a playroom to hang out with another researcher while the mothers were asked to perform a task: they were to deliver a speech about their strengths and weaknesses. There was one important difference between Rachel's and Sara's tasks, however: while Rachel was to give the speech in front of a group of angry judges, Sara was to give the speech in front of . . . no one.

If you were a fly on the wall, you would have observed Sara cheerfully chatting to herself while Rachel spoke to a handful of unhappy evaluators. They appeared to be annoyed; they kept shaking their heads, huffing and puffing. Unsurprisingly, at the end of the ordeal, the sensors indicated that Rachel was sweating and her heartbeat had accelerated, while Sara's physiological recordings were stable.

Stressed Rachel was then reunited with little baby Roni, and relaxed Susan rejoined tiny baby Sara. Would the infants' heart rates alter in response to their mothers'? Although the children did not witness their moms delivering their respective speeches, their physiology changed rapidly, as if they themselves had given the address. Roni's heart rate went up by six beats per minute after reuniting with stressed Rachel, while Sara's went down by four beats per minute after reuniting with relaxed Susan.* Although the children were not consciously aware of their parent's emotions, they felt those emotions in their own bodies immediately. Their physiology aligned with that of their caregivers.

This transfer of emotions enabled Roni and Sara to learn from their mothers about the type of environment they were in— whether it was a dangerous one that required caution or an embracing one that should be explored. Indeed, it was not only the babies' physiology that changed upon their reunions; their behavior was affected, too. After reuniting with her mother, Sara (and the other infants of moms who experienced the stress-free condition) was happy to engage with the other researchers on the team, while Roni (and the other infants of moms who experienced the stressful condition) turned away from them, avoiding eye contact. Roni seemed to have learned that he should be careful of others in the lab, while Sara absorbed the notion that others were to be trusted.

Emotions—which are, in essence, bodily reactions to external events or internal thoughts—travel from one person to the other, delivering with them important messages. In Mendes's study, the focus was on information traveling from mother to child, but, of course, messages travel the other way, too. When a child cries, a parent will instantly feel the pain and be driven to reduce it by helping the youngster.

How does emotional transfer work? How does your smile generate joy in me? How does your frown create anger in my own

---

* Roni and Sara are representative of the other babies in the experiment; that is, the statistics given here are an average of the other babies' reactions.

mind? There are two main routes. The first is unconscious mimicry. You may have heard of how people constantly mimic other people's gestures, sounds, and facial expressions. We do this automatically— if you move your eyebrows slightly upward, I will likely do the same; if you huff, I am more likely to puff. When someone's body is expressing stress, we are more likely to tighten up ourselves because of mimicry and, as a result, feel stress in our own bodies. The second route does not rely on mimicry but is simply a reaction to emotional stimuli. The idea here is quite simple. Because a fearful face often indicates that there is something to be afraid of, we react to it with fear—just as we would react to someone wielding a large ax swiftly moving our way.

The Amygdala of the Internet

As it turns out, we do not even need to observe people for their emotions to ripple in. Posts on social media will do the trick. Take an infamous Facebook experiment.[15] In January 2012, Facebook manipulated the news feeds of over half a million users so that some users saw a large number of positive posts in their feed, while others encountered a large number of negative posts. The Facebook researchers found that users who saw more positive posts, such as images of people embracing, posted more positive messages themselves. Those who saw more negative posts, such as complaints about service in a restaurant, created more negative posts on their wall. True, we do not know how the people who posted were feeling, but we can say that positive and negative messages travel fast online. The experiment did not go down well with Facebook users, who were angry that the company experimented on them without their knowledge.

A couple of years later, another group of researchers decided to prove the same point, this time with Twitter.[16] To avoid the ethical issues present in the Facebook experiment, they simply observed people's feeds instead of manipulating them. This setup does not allow for conclusions about cause and effect. However, the researchers found that when a person posted an uplifting tweet, their feed just prior probably included about 4 percent more positive tweets than negative. If a person posted a downer, their feed just prior probably had about 4 percent more negative tweets than positive.

If you are an avid Twitter user, beware: tweeting is one of the most emotionally arousing activities you likely engage in on most days. Forget exercise—studies show that tweeting raises your pulse, makes you sweat, and enlarges your pupils—all indicators of arousal.[17] Relative to just browsing the Web, tweeting and retweeting enhances brain activity indicative of emotional arousal by 75 percent. Simply reading your feed increases your emotional arousal by 65 percent.* I'd always suspected that Twitter was the "amygdala of the Internet." It has all the required ingredients for this role: messages are fast, short, and transferred broadly. These instinctive aspects of Twitter will call upon our emotional system many times, bypassing our much-needed filters (what Daniel Kahneman famously refers to as our "fast" and "slow" thinking).[18] While the tool can be helpful in transmitting valuable information, it may also encourage the less measured aspects of our nature.

You may think of your emotions as part of a private process that happens inside you. Remember, though, that your feelings leak out and are absorbed by others near and far. The consequences can be significant. Not only are you affecting other people's well-being, you are also affecting their actions, because mood affects behavior.

---

* Note that these studies were funded by Twitter for its own purposes and were not peer-reviewed.

We already saw how a mother's emotion quickly influences her baby's behavior, but this can happen between two unrelated adults, too.

In one study, groups of students were asked to complete a task together.[19] Unbeknownst to the students, the experimenter had inserted a confederate within each group—a drama student, who was instructed to act as if he was either in a good mood or a bad mood. Not surprisingly, the drama student's emotions quickly altered the mood of the others. But it did not end there. Mood did not just affect mood; it also affected behavior. Groups in which the

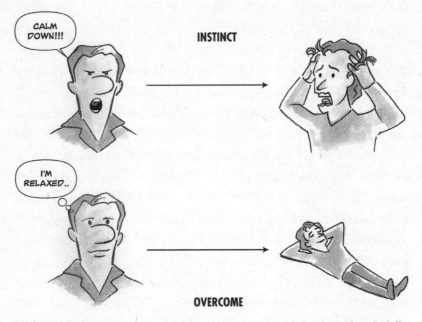

Figure 2.1. Emotion. *Your emotions are contagious—use them thoughtfully. Our intuition tells us that our emotions are private. That instinct is wrong. Others absorb your feelings instantly, constantly, and unconsciously, and it influences their actions. Be mindful that you are inducing emotions in others simply by experiencing them yourself. For example, when a parent is stressed, a child learns to be less trusting of people around them and becomes less social. Although it's not always an easy task, a parent can try to regulate their emotions before interacting with their child.*

confederate acted as if he was happy performed better, were more likely to cooperate, and experienced less conflict. Groups in which the confederate acted as if he was in a bad mood performed the task much worse.

It is important, then, to be mindful that we are altering people's emotions simply by experiencing feelings ourselves. Similarly, other people's emotions change our own state—we are constantly synchronizing with each other and everyone around us.

Is My Brain Like Yours?

For synchronization to take place, it helps if you and your conversation partner share similar brains and bodies. I tend to think this is why identical twins often feel they have a metaphysical connection. As a result of sharing the exact same genes and many life experiences, their bodies and brains are physically alike. Subsequently, they often respond to their environment in comparable ways. When they are viewing the same film or when listening to someone talking, their brain patterns will be in sync. As a result, it is easy for one to predict how the other is feeling, what the other is thinking, and what they will say next—one twin simply uses their own intentions, feelings, and thoughts as a proxy.

You do not need to be one half of identical twins, however, for considerable neural synchronization to occur with another person. In fact, there is some evidence that your brain may align with a very distant relative of yours—the monkey. Imagine you are sitting in your living room at the end of the day with a cold beer in your hand, watching your favorite childhood film, *The Jungle Book*. Next to you on the sofa sits your human buddy Lenny. Beside him sits your long-tailed macaque, George. Both Lenny and George are recovering from long days at the lab and are happy to relax in front of the animated feature with you. How similar do you think your pattern of neural activity is to that of your buddy Lenny while you both watch the film? And how similar is it to that of your hairy macaque, George? Take a guess: when will synchronization between the three of you be particularly strong and when will it break down?

Although this exact study has not yet been conducted, a somewhat analogous one has.[20] Eye movements of humans and monkeys were recorded while they watched segments of three films on mute: a BBC nature documentary on the lives of mammals, Charlie Chaplin's *City Lights*, and *The Jungle Book*. Eye-movement patterns are not the same as neural patterns, but they give us an indication of what viewers are attending to at every point in time. So how similar are humans' and monkeys' eye movements while they watch the same movie?

On average, your pattern of eye movements will overlap with a monkey's 31 percent of the time. About a third of the time, you and Mr. Macaque will be looking at the same point on the screen.* The data showed that the moments in which synchronization was particularly strong were the ones in which people or animals appeared in the movie. Many of these instances were ones in which faces and eyes were clearly visible—both humans and monkeys focused on those. We know from brain-imaging studies that the amygdala responds strongly to faces, and particularly to eyes.[21] These are salient stimuli, and so they elicit an arousal response, especially when those faces convey an emotional expression. This is probably why marketers often include faces in advertisements and websites—they are hoping to grab (human) attention.

---

* The scientist made sure that these similarities could not be explained by a simple pattern of visual features such as bright colors.

What about your friend Lenny? If you watch a film and your friend Lenny is watching the same film, your pattern of eye movements will overlap, on average, 65 percent of the time. Consider this: if you were to watch a film on Monday and then watch the exact same film again on Thursday, 70 percent of the time your eyes would follow a similar pattern in scanning the screen. In other words, the amount of overlap in how *you* view the film on two separate occasions is similar to the variation in how you and Lenny view the film. What this study suggests is that the brains of seemingly different humans and even of nonhumans react in a relatively similar manner, especially in response to cues that trigger emotion or arousal and in response to narratives (such as movies).

When we are sitting in an auditorium listening to a speech, or in a movie theater watching a film, or at home reading a book, we are not aware that the neural storm in our minds is similar to that of other people who have watched this movie, heard this speech, or read this book. This does not mean that there are no individual differences—it would be ludicrous to suggest so. There are, indeed, diverse neural fingerprints in all of us. And yet a large proportion of our behavior can be explained by commonalities, not differences. When conducting experiments in the lab, I am often amazed by how similar people are in responding to questions and performing tasks, especially when those tasks involve emotional or social factors. In many cases, 80 percent of people's responses can be predicted by the average response and only about 20 percent are accounted for by individual differences. The neural hurricane in your head right now is remarkably like that of other readers scanning this exact sentence, even if they are reading it in a different language.

In life, we tend to focus on our differences, because those carry the most amount of information about what makes each person unique. We forget that while people sometimes look and sound different from us, our brains are organized in a very similar way and will react similarly given the same stimulation.

The similarity of the machinery of our minds may not be an easy notion to accept, because from our point of view—from inside our skull—our mental world feels completely unique. It is difficult to imagine that others around us share very similar neural patterns of activity—and, therefore, similar mental states, thoughts, and feelings. How could this other person outside of me be so much like me? Yet the basic architecture of our brains is remarkably similar, often generating similar reactions when we are experiencing the same events and stimuli.

The great benefit of sharing similar brain function and structure is that it makes it easier for us to communicate ideas, which means that we need not navigate the world on our own. One of the most powerful ways to communicate ideas effectively is to share feelings. Emotions are especially contagious; by expressing feelings ourselves we are shaping other people's emotional states, and by doing so we make it more likely that the people in front of us will take on our point of view. But will any type of emotion work? Should you elicit laughter or fear? Hope or dread? In the next chapter we will answer these questions.

3

⸻◈⸻

Should You Scare People into Action?
(Incentives)

Moving with Pleasure and Freezing with Fear

E mployees must wash their hands!" You encounter such signs in the restrooms of most bars and restaurants. Have you ever wondered if workers obey these orders? The Centers for Disease Control and Prevention (CDC) did. To find out, CDC health workers visited hundreds of food joints across the United States and openly recorded employees' hygiene practices. (I suggest you take a seat before reading further.) Turns out, a whopping 62 percent of employees fail to wash their hands. This is a serious problem. Each year in the United States alone, sixty thousand people are hospitalized after eating at a restaurant or deli due to a foodborne disease that might have been prevented by better hygiene practices.[1]

I would have liked to tell you that the problem is specific to kitchen workers; maybe something about the enchanting smell of lamb stew distracts people from handwashing. But, unfortunately, the problem extends well beyond kitchens. Let's take a look at hospitals. Sanitization in medical settings is extremely important for preventing the spread of disease. Medical staffs are repeatedly made aware of the severity of the situation, and warning signs are placed alongside sanitization-gel dispensers. Unfortunately, however, compliance rates at your local medical center are probably not much higher than at your neighborhood fast-food joint. The average reported compliance rate for hand hygiene in medical centers is about 38.7 percent, not far off the 38 percent compliance rate reported for restaurants.[2] And it is not just medical staff members and cooks who skip scrubbing their hands. According to a study from Michigan State University, only 5 percent of the population at large cleans their hands properly (that is, with soap and water for at least fifteen seconds) after using a public bathroom.[3]

How, then, do you get people to wash their hands? The solution uncovers surprising clues about what motivates people and can be traced back to the structural organization of the human brain.

Good Shift!

In 2008, a group of researchers from New York State embarked on an ambitious program.[4] They had twenty-four months and $50,000 to significantly enhance hand sanitization in hospitals. An intensive care unit (ICU) in the northeastern United States was chosen for a case study. The unit was already equipped with easy-to-use sanitization-gel dispensers, sinks in every room, and signs everywhere reminding medical staffers that they must wash their hands. Yet compliance was alarmingly low.

What could be done? The team brainstormed for weeks, after

which they went out and purchased twenty-one video surveillance cameras. The cameras were carefully installed in the ICU pointing toward the gel dispensers and sinks. The plan was to transmit the recordings live via the Web to India, where twenty auditors would monitor the actions of the medical staff twenty-four/seven to determine the rate of sanitization. Doorway motion sensors would alert the auditors back in India every time a staff member entered or left a patient's room. This was not a "nanny cam" situation, since the medical staff was well aware that they were being watched. Shockingly, however, even though they knew they were being recorded, only one in ten staff members complied with the handwashing rules. That meant that surveillance alone was not enough. The team had to come up with something better. Luckily, they had a plan.

What they did next would change the staff's behavior almost instantly. The researchers placed an electronic board in each room giving the staff immediate feedback on how they were doing. Every time a doctor, nurse, or other worker washed their hands, the numbers on the board went up. These figures indicated how well the current shift was going: what percentage of workers were currently washing their hands and what the weekly rate was. What happened? Compliance soared to almost 90 percent!

These results are astonishing. In fact, they are so unbelievable that most scientists would treat them with suspicion. So the researchers set out to replicate their results in another division in the hospital. Sure enough, the same findings were observed.[5] In the second division, one in three medical staff members sanitized their hands before the electronic board was installed, a rate closer to the national average. Then the electronic feedback was introduced and—boom! Compliance rose once again, to about 90 percent.

Why does this intervention work so well? To resolve this

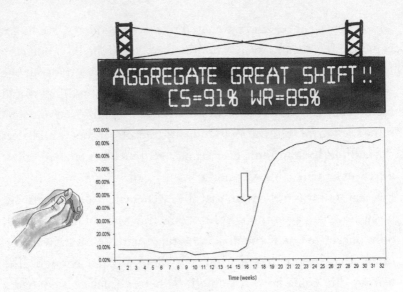

Figure 3.1. *Motivating medical staff members to sanitize their hands with immediate positive feedback rather than threats. Staff compliance in an ICU started at 10 percent and shot up to almost 90 percent once the live-feedback electronic board was installed.*

mystery, we need to think about what was different in the team's approach. What did the New York researchers do in this ICU in the northeastern United States that no one else was doing?

Anticipation of Pleasure and Pain

The great eighteenth-century polymath Jeremy Bentham begins his most influential work with this statement: "Nature has placed mankind under the governance of two sovereign masters, *pain* and *pleasure*. It is for them alone to point out what *we ought to do*, as well as to determine *what we shall do*. . . . They govern us in all we do, in all we say, in all we think."[6]

I take some liberty in assuming that Bentham used the terms "pain" and "pleasure" broadly to describe both bad and good feelings. "Pleasure," or a positive emotion, can be attained from a range of stimuli and occurrences: from material rewards, affection, recognition, admiration, hope—and we seek out these experiences repeatedly. Likewise, we are motivated to dodge both physical and emotional pain. We try to escape sickness and bullying, avoid losing a loved one or a possession. The list goes on.

It is not surprising, then, that when we try to get others to act, we often offer a reward (you can think of this as a material or emotional "carrot") or warn of a loss (you can think of this as a material or emotional "stick"). Promising an employee a promotion if they work longer hours is a carrot. So is telling your partner you love them after they wash the dishes. Threatening your child with punishment if they do not complete their homework is a stick, as is telling a patient that they must start exercising or risk ill health.

The brilliance of the electronic board at the ICU was that instead of using a threat, the common approach in this situation, the researchers chose a positive strategy. Warning the staff about the spread of disease is the standard "stick" strategy. The research team, however, was offering "carrots"—immediate rewards in the form of positive feedback.* Every time a staff member washed their hands, the numbers on the board went up, accompanied by a positive personalized comment, such as "You are doing great!" Anticipating the warm and fuzzy feeling that comes with such immediate positive feedback drove the employees to do something they would otherwise not do as often (sanitize their hands), and after a while it became a habit. Studies find that immediate positive feedback need not continue forever in order for people to maintain the desired behavior. Even after its removal, people will often continue

---

* This was not the only brilliant aspect of the approach. The electronic board also provided an indication of social norms—what other people were doing—as well as competition between shifts. The importance of social learning is discussed in chapter 7.

with the same action for a significant amount of time, simply because it has become ingrained in their behavioral repertoire.

This is surprising. You would think that the possibility of spreading disease, infecting ourselves and others, would be a strong enough motivator to induce action. Such logic is what leads us to try to change others' behavior with fear. Yet inconsequential positive feedback drove action much more effectively than warnings or threats. It may seem odd, but it fits well with what we know about the brain. When it comes to eliciting action, immediate rewards can often be more effective than future punishment. To understand why, we first need to learn about the law of approach and avoidance.

The Law of Approach and Avoidance

Imagine you wake up one fine morning to discover that the physical rules governing your world have been altered overnight. No warning was issued in advance. In fact, when you turned in the previous night, there was no clue of what was about to occur. Per your normal routine, you had a quick read of your preferred news source, then placed your smartphone on the nightstand and turned off the lights.

When you arise eight hours later and reach to grab your phone, something bizarre occurs—an event you have never before experienced. The moment your arm stretches toward the blinking piece of metal, it bounces off the table. You get up, in an attempt to catch the escaping hardware, but the faster you run, the faster it escapes. Once out through the bedroom doorway, it rolls down the corridor and into the kitchen. "Hmmm," you think, "I wonder if this is one of those bizarre hacking cases you hear about. Maybe someone broke into my phone and is now controlling it from afar with a large magnet!"

You figure it is best to clear your head before investigating further. So you enter the bathroom to wash your face. You are distracted and by mistake turn on the hot water. But when you jump back to avoid the boiling drops from burning you, they move *toward* you, landing on your puzzled face. And when you reach out for the towel, the large white cloth moves *away*.

It is as if, like Alice through the looking glass, you've entered an alternative universe. Which laws have been altered? Can you figure it out? And if so, can your brain flexibly adapt to the new rules of an environment it was not evolved to exist in? Or are we hardwired to interact with the physical world our ancestors colonized?

In 1986, the psychologist Wayne Hershberger carried out an ingenious experiment to test just that. He physically built an environment where a basic tenet we all live by—the law of approach and avoidance—was reversed.[7] This principle, which guides our everyday behavior, is nearly as basic as gravity. It's so rudimentary, in fact, that articulating it sounds as astute as saying that the sun rises in the morning and sets at night. Yet here I go.

The law of approach and avoidance states that we approach those people, items, and events we believe can do us good and avoid those that can do us harm. In other words, we execute actions to bring us closer to a piece of cherry pie, a loved one, or a promotion, and we distance ourselves from an allergen, a bad relationship, or a failing project. We move toward pleasure and away from pain.

While you've probably never contemplated this elementary rule of behavior before, you should. Because what we are about to see is that while we do not attempt to catch the sunset at eight a.m. or the sunrise at eight p.m., we often, unconsciously, defy the law of approach and avoidance when trying to influence others. And while the laws of behavior are not as deterministic as those of physics, attempting to work against them leaves us at a disadvantage when trying to induce an action. But I'm jumping ahead.

Let's turn back to Hershberger's brilliant experiment. Hershberger wanted to know whether we are born with a basic tendency to move toward the good and away from the bad. Is the brain literally wired such that the pursuit of pleasure is linked with forward action? If so, are we able to reverse this pairing if needed? In other words, he wanted to know what would happen if avoiding fire required moving closer to the flame. This is not merely a theoretical conundrum. There are instances when gaining what you want involves moving away from it. Consider, for example, the need to let go of a flaky romantic partner so that the space between you will eventually cause that person to miss you and come running back; or think of a firefighter who runs toward a fire in order to save lives.

To investigate the law of approach and avoidance, Hershberger turned to chicks—the type with two wings and a beak. He gathered forty tiny yellow chicks that had just hatched. One by one, the newborn chicks were put on a straight runway containing a cup of food. Immediately upon seeing the cup, all the chicks started moving toward it. Although they were fresh to the world, they were born knowing that moving toward food is necessary to obtain it. This is when Hershberger played his little trick. When the chicks moved toward the cup, Hershberger moved it away at twice the speed. The faster the chick toddled toward the nourishment, the faster the food escaped. In this strange new world, approach was not the answer for getting what you want. (See figure 3.2, on next page.)

How then would they obtain the seeds? When the chicks moved away from the food, Hershberger moved the cup toward

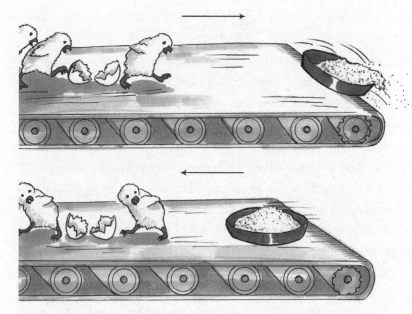

Figure 3.2. *Approach behavior is difficult to unlearn. When chicks on a treadmill moved toward a plate of grain, the plate moved farther away. The chicks failed to learn that to obtain the grain, they had to distance themselves from the plate.*

them at twice the speed. So to get the yummy seeds, the chicks needed to learn a relatively simple rule: distance yourself from what you would like to obtain and it will follow you. Although the chicks were ravenous and motivated to solve the puzzle, they could not overcome the instinct to move toward the prize. The problem was that the new rule defied the environment their brains were equipped to handle. As many opportunities as they received, they were unable to overcome the strong tendency to approach the trophy, even when that meant never obtaining it. They remained famished.

This study was one of the first to indicate that animals are born with a built-in behavioral schema of approach and avoidance. But what does this mean for humans?

Go, No Go

Humans are a bit like chicks. We, too, have a bias to move toward objects of pleasure and away from objects of pain, because that is usually effective. The bias runs deep. Our brains are wired such that anticipating a reward not only triggers approach, it is more likely to elicit action altogether. The fear of a loss, on the other hand, is more likely to elicit *in*action. This asymmetry partially explains why positive feedback was more successful at making the medical staffers wash their hands (an approach behavior) than threatening them with illness; biologically, we are wired such that anticipation of good things elicits action.

Consider an experiment my collaborators and I conducted a few years back at University College London.[8] The study was led by the neuroscientist and psychiatrist Marc Guitart-Masip, who is now at the Karolinska Institutet in Sweden. One of the participants in Marc's experiment was Edvard, a well-educated, meticulously dressed Norwegian. Edvard was seated in front of a computer and asked to place his fingers gently on the space bar. His job was relatively easy: he would be presented with one of four images on the screen—let's say, a painting by Klee, another by Picasso, a third by Kandinsky, and a fourth by Matisse.* Every time Edvard saw the Klee painting, he was supposed to press the space bar as quickly as possible in order to earn one dollar. I will call this condition "act and you'll be rewarded." No surprise, Edvard was quick to press the space bar to get a dollar every time the Klee painting appeared on the screen—just as the medical staff members at the ICU were quick to wash their hands when leaving a patient's room to up their

---

* In reality, the stimuli used were abstract images.

score on the electronic board. But would Edvard do as well when he had to press a button to avoid a loss?

When the Picasso painting appeared on the screen, Edvard again was told to press a button as quickly as possible. This time, however, hitting the space key did not gain him a dollar but, instead, ensured that he would avoid losing one. I will call this condition "work to avoid harm." This situation is equivalent to washing your hands to avoid catching an infection, or a failing student being assigned an extra project to avoid being kicked out of class. It is a "Go" strategy to dodge a loss. Edvard was able to learn the rule, but 30 percent of participants in the study were not. That's not all. Like most other participants in the study, Edvard was slower to press the space key to avoid losing a dollar than he was to press it in order to gain a dollar. He was also more likely to miss pressing the key altogether, just like the medical staffers who often skipped sanitizing their hands. Why is this?

The human brain is built to associate "forward" action with a reward, not with avoiding harm, because that is often (but not always) the most useful response. The situation in which Edvard found himself defied the law of "approach and avoidance." When we are faced with the possibility of acquiring something good, our brains trigger a chain of biological events that makes us more likely to act fast. This is known as the brain's "Go" response, and it involves signals that originate in a region deep in the brain known as the midbrain. The signals move up the brain to the striatum, near the center of the brain, and finally to regions in the frontal cortex that control motor responses.

In contrast, when we are anticipating something bad, our instinct is to withdraw. The brain triggers a "No Go" reaction. These "No Go" signals also originate deep in the midbrain and move up the brain to the striatum and the frontal cortex. But unlike "Go" signals, they *inhibit* a response. As a result, we are more likely to execute an action when we are anticipating something good than when we are anticipating something bad.[9]

Hope for Action

If you want someone to act quickly, promising a reward that elicits an anticipation of pleasure may be better than threatening them with a punishment that elicits an anticipation of pain. Whether you are trying to motivate your team to work harder or your child to tidy their room, remember the brain's "Go" reaction. Creating positive anticipation in others—perhaps a weekly acknowledgment on the company website of the most productive employee or the possibility of finding a beloved toy under a pile of clothing—may be more effective at motivating action than the threat of a pay cut or a time-out.

Take, for example, a woman I met recently—let's call her Cherry. Cherry came up to me after a talk I gave at her company to share her experience. For a long time, she had been trying to persuade her husband to visit their local gym. Unlike her, he was not a big fan of exercise. In an attempt to change his ways, she politely mentioned his growing paunch. It did not work. She warned him of the elevated risk of heart disease for people who do not exercise—also to no avail. Then, one night after her husband came back from a rare visit to the gym, she complimented him on his defined muscles. The next day, he went again. As long as she made her increasing physical attraction to him clear, he kept going back, again and again and again. A slight change in Cherry's feedback—from emphasizing the possible long-term negative consequences of not exercising to emphasizing immediate positive consequences—made all the difference.

At another event, a senior manager of a very successful business approached me to share his story. I'll call him Sam. A few years back, Sam had been faced with a problem that could have lost him millions of dollars. A client threatened to take his business elsewhere unless Sam was able to cut 20 percent from the cost of the client's project within a month. The pressure was on, and Sam had to get his team working full force on a solution. He could have approached his team the way most people would. That would go something like this: "Listen, guys, we have a serious problem here. Our client is threatening to leave and take his millions with him if we do not find a way to cut the project's budget by twenty percent pronto. So let's get started and put everything we have into making sure this does not happen." But he chose a different approach: "Right, guys, we have been given a challenge. We need to find ways to cut the budget of our client's project by twenty percent so that we can retain him and make millions. I wrote our goal in big letters on the board in the common room. We will update our progress every day as we go along. Let's do this." According to Sam, it worked like magic. The team was energized. They tracked their progress on the board, got a kick out of every advance, and ended up overshooting their target.

Here is another example, one that is becoming more relevant in this social media age: crowdfunding requests. Crowdfunding websites are those where individuals appeal for funds from other individuals. Usually an appeal includes a photo and a short paragraph describing the request. Consider two such appeals. The first is accompanied by a photo of a happy young woman glittering in sunlight. This woman has become severely ill and requires costly medical treatment. The second request is accompanied by a photo of a guy lying limp on a hospital bed, tubes running in and out of his body, desperation in his eyes. He, too, has fallen ill and requires costly medical treatment. Which do you think is more likely to receive funding?

Alexander Genevsky and Brian Knutson from Stanford University examined 13,500 online requests for funding.[10] They found that appeals that included photos that elicit positive feelings, especially those portraying smiling individuals, were more likely to be funded than those supplemented by negative images. This is surprising, considering how often charitable requests are accompanied by aversive images. The photo of the patient in the hospital may indeed elicit compassion, but it also triggers an instinctive reaction to distance ourselves from the anguish and look away. In contrast, in response to positive images, people experience an "approach reaction," and they engage. An image of a healthy and happy individual makes it easy to envision the possibility for progress toward recovery, which motivates people to help. An image of a sick individual makes it difficult to imagine a happy ending, often resulting in passivity.

Genevsky and Knutson wanted to know if they could predict which crowdfunding appeals would be successful and which would be ignored. They gathered lots of data, including the amount requested and how many words were used in the post; they asked a group of people to rate how the requests made them feel; and they recorded the brain activity of twenty-eight individuals while they considered the appeals. The researchers found that the best way to predict the success of an online appeal was to look at the response of the nucleus accumbens. The nucleus accumbens is the part of the brain that processes feelings of pleasure; it is sometimes referred to as the "reward center" of the brain, because it signals anticipation of upcoming rewards. If the nucleus accumbens was firing strongly while people considered a request, then that request was likely to be funded on the website. Looking at the brain activity in the nucleus accumbens of a small group of volunteers was the best predictor of how thousands of others would react online, better than simply asking the volunteers whether they would be willing to fund said requests or how they were feeling. Sometimes examining the brain directly can give us a purer indication of what is going on inside someone's mind than asking that person to introspect.

Freezing in the Middle of the Road

Sam the manager, Cherry the wife, and the research team at the ICU all offered rewards, either material or nonmaterial, instead of warnings. In all these incidents, pairing requests for action with positive outcomes, rather than threats, was important for inducing change. What happens, though, when your aim is to have people avoid acting?

Let's go back to our experiment to find out. When either a Kandinsky or a Matisse painting was presented on screen, Edvard was supposed to do nothing. If he did nothing after observing a Kandinsky, he would earn a dollar. This is like a schoolteacher praising a student for sitting quietly in class. In contrast, doing nothing after observing a Matisse would guarantee that Edvard would avoid losing a dollar. This situation is equivalent to a student sitting quietly in class in order to avoid being punished by the schoolteacher. Again, Edvard performed well, but he was slightly better at remaining still to avoid a loss than he was at remaining still to gain a reward. This is because when faced with the possibility of a loss, a "No Go" response is triggered in the brain, inhibiting action.

This means that when your goal is to cause someone else not to do something—a child to avoid eating a cookie or an employee to avoid communicating confidential information to unauthorized individuals—warning of bad consequences may be more effective than promising rewards. In fact, immediate threats can cause us to freeze altogether.

You might be familiar with the concept of a deer freezing in headlights. Well, we too freeze when we are afraid. The other day I was crossing a busy street in Boston. Constantly dividing my time between the United States and the United Kingdom, I frequently turn to look the wrong way before attempting to curve my way through traffic. This confusion had gotten me into trouble on more than one occasion. This time, I was crossing a major road, turning my head left when I should have turned it right. Halfway through the crosswalk, I saw a vehicle heading my way from the unexpected direction with worrying speed. Alarm bells sounded inside my head; fear took over. In my mind's eye, I could see myself flattened by the moving car like pizza dough. My first reaction was to stop short. For a split second I froze, right there in the middle of the road. Only after I regained my senses could I escape. I made it to the other side unharmed, but one can imagine a situation where those few lost milliseconds would have made a big difference.

Why would evolution equip us with a freezing reaction? To answer that question, we need to think back to a time when our number one goal was to escape predators. To avoid being chewed up by a lion or tiger, we had three options: (a) run away as fast as we could, (b) fight back as hard as possible, or (c) remain perfectly still. Why would we want to remain still? Well, if we do not move, we may go undetected. Humans and other animals are really good at detecting motion, even from the corners of their eyes, so staying still when our life is threatened may save us. The second reason for freezing is pretending to be dead.* Many predators will avoid eating dead animals, as they can cause sickness. In fact, national park rangers advise campers to pretend to be dead if they are ever

---

* Analysis of recent terrorist acts, such as the shootings at a theater in Paris and a club in Orlando, revealed that while some individuals had indeed survived the shooting by playing dead, in other instances the shooter in apparent rage fired at victims believed to be dead.

attacked by a black bear. Playing dead can be a good strategy for getting left alone, which is one reason we have inherited a freezing reaction to fear that often precedes the "fight or flight" response.[11]

Survivors of plane crashes will often describe passengers sitting in their seats, frozen, overtaken by fear and shock, rather than trying to escape. Their behavior resembles that of mice in the lab. If you train a mouse to associate a specific sound with the delivery of an electric shock, you will observe the mouse freezing whenever it hears that sound, in anticipation of the upcoming pain. Sometimes you will see this reaction even if the mouse has an escape route. The freezing reaction is generated by the amygdala, a small structure deep in the brain that is involved in processing emotion.[12] If, however, you train the mouse to associate a specific sound with the arrival of something good (like an attractive mouse of the other sex), you will observe the mouse moving around its chamber with jittery excitement—demonstrating the relationship between expectation of reward and action.*

Fear and anxiety, in many instances, will cause us to withdraw, to freeze, to give up, rather than take action. I'm not saying this is always the case, but you'll likely notice the response often if you pay attention. That, however, is not the only reason why the ICU staffers were not swayed to sanitize their hands by the threat of

---

* Some of you may be wondering how this relates to the phenomenon of "loss aversion." Loss aversion is the tendency of people, when given a choice, to choose to avoid a loss rather than attain a reward. In other words, when making a decision (such as whether to invest in a stock), people will put more weight on what they may lose than what they may gain. The existence of "loss aversion" does not, however, translate to increased action in the face of a possible loss as compared to a possible gain. The few studies that have been interpreted in such a way could, in fact, be explained otherwise. For example, in one study, a group of teachers were given $4,000 and told that the money would be taken away if their students' grades did not improve. The teachers in another group were promised $4,000 if their students' grades improved. The former group performed better. While this study has been interpreted as showing the impact of fear on motivation, you could also think about the results as reflecting the impact of immediate rewards—$4,000 in pocket—over future ones.

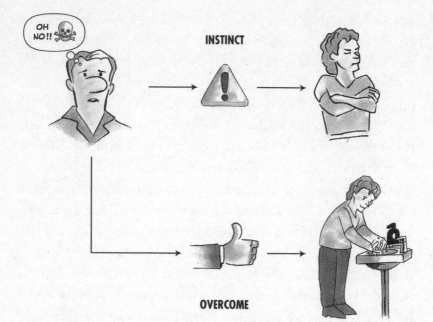

Figure 3.3. Incentives. *Induce action using positive strategies instead of warnings and threats. Often our instinct is to try to alter people's actions by warning of future dangers. The strategy frequently fails, because fear can demotivate people and lead them to freeze up rather than act. We can overcome our instinct and instead use positive strategies to change behavior, such as by offering immediate rewards. The anticipation of rewards, even simple positive feedback or an online "like," can trigger the brain's "go" response. For example, warning medical staff members that they must wash their hands to prevent the spread of disease did not affect their behavior. However, upping their scores every time they sanitized their hands did.*

disease, or why the possibility of obesity was not enough to get Cherry's husband to hit the gym. There is another reason: *immediacy.*

Give It to Me Now!

Have you ever heard the phrase "don't eat the marshmallow"? There are few studies in psychology famous enough to have become part of our everyday lexicon. A 1988 study by Walter Mischel, a professor of psychology at Columbia University, is one of them. Mischel and his colleagues, who were at Stanford University at the time, published an article in the *Journal of Personality and Social Psychology* under the unassuming title "The Nature of Adolescent Competencies Predicted by Preschool Delay of Gratification."[13] Most of you would have heard of it simply as "the marshmallow study." The study is portrayed as a demonstration of the importance of self-control for success. (In fact, Mischel subsequently wrote a book titled *The Marshmallow Test: Why Self-Control Is the Engine of Success*.) However, that popular interpretation may not be the full story. I believe there is more to the marshmallow study than meets the eye. But first, let me briefly recount the original experiment before offering a new lesson we can take away from that study.

In the late 1960s, Mischel contacted the administrators of the Bing Nursery School at Stanford University to inquire whether their preschoolers would consider participating in an experiment. They agreed. The children, aged four to six, were brought into a room one by one and seated in front of a table. At the center of the table was a delicious treat, such as a cookie or a marshmallow. Imagine, for example, little Peter. Peter is a talkative preschooler. Like many other preschoolers, he has a special fondness for moving vehicles—trains, tractors, planes, everyday cars. He is also especially fond of sugary treats, including, yes, marshmallows. Peter walks into the room, and his attention is immediately captured by the pinkish squishy treat waiting to be relished. The experimenter informs Peter that he has to leave for a short while to check on another kid, Allen. In the meantime, Peter can eat the marshmallow if he wants. However, if he waits for the experimenter's return, he will receive not one but two marshmallows!

Peter is left unaccompanied. What will he do? Many kids wait for the researcher to return with the second marshmallow; only then do they consume both. It is not easy for them, though. The kids adopt different strategies to distract themselves from the prize. Some place their hands under their little bums to ensure that their fingers will not find their way to the mushy treat. Others distract themselves by reciting nursery rhymes. Why is it so difficult for the children to avoid eating the marshmallow?

Think back to Marc Guitart-Masip's go/no go experiment. We now know that the brain elicits a "go" response in anticipation of a reward. Peter, however, had to engage in a "no go" response to obtain a reward. Just like Edvard, who had to avoid pressing a computer key when viewing the Kandinsky painting in order to receive a dollar, Peter had to avoid acting in order to receive the marshmallow. That's not easy, especially for a four-year-old, since the child's brain has not fully developed circuits to bypass these instincts. What's more, the brain treats an immediate marshmallow as worth more than a future marshmallow. The part of the brain that signals rewards—the nucleus accumbens—produces a larger signal when we consider rewards that are attainable at the moment relative to ones that will be attainable sometime in the future.[14] "Now" is often worth more than "later." Mischel's study shows that while the kids find it taxing, many manage to overcome their instinct and wait for the two future marshmallows.

I strongly suspect that millions of parents have placed their children in front of a yummy treat and promised them a bigger, better one if they can forgo temptation for fifteen minutes. I believe this to be true because of what Mischel discovered next. A decade later, Mischel contacted the preschoolers' parents; the children were by now teenagers. He asked the parents a series of questions, including how well their children were doing academically, socially, and mentally. The kids who had been able to delay gratification a decade earlier—those who'd waited for the second marshmallow— were doing better in almost all domains as teenagers. Mischel's conclusion was that the children who'd waited for the second marshmallow had a stronger ability for self-control, and this enabled them to excel in many domains.[15] That, however, is only one possible explanation. There is another interpretation for why some kids postponed gratification while others did not: the children's expectations of the future.

The Future Is Uncertain

Remember Peter? The talkative, train-loving preschooler? Well, Peter did not wait for the second marshmallow. Shortly after the researcher left, he reached out for the light pink morsel and stuffed it into his mouth. "Poor self-control," you may say. Perhaps. Here is another thought: maybe Peter was not fully convinced that the researcher would come back with a second marshmallow. This is not an unreasonable assumption. The researcher may forget, or he may be lying. An even worse scenario crosses Peter's mind: maybe he won't even get to eat the one marshmallow that is in front of him if he waits too long. Again, this possibility should not be ruled out. Perhaps the researcher will run out of marshmallows, and Peter will need to share his with Allen, the other preschooler. There is no point in waiting restlessly for fifteen minutes, he concludes. In fact, it may be better to eat the one marshmallow in the hand rather than wait for the two marshmallows in the bush. Peter does not necessarily have low self-control; he may just be less trusting of others, or less optimistic. Both of these reasons could explain why Peter made the choice he did and why he grew up the way he did afterward. Sociability and optimism have been shown to significantly affect how our lives unfold, with more social and optimistic individuals doing better in life, on average.[16]

This additional interpretation of the marshmallow study has been supported by an experiment conducted at the University of Rochester. The researchers in Rochester set out to change kids' beliefs of how reliable the experimenter was before giving them the marshmallow test.[17] This is how they did it: they invited children between three and five years old into an art room and gave them a create-your-own-cup kit. The children could use the kit to decorate a blank paper slip that would then be inserted into a special cup. They were also given a set of old crayons in a box that was very difficult to open and told that if they could wait for a few moments, the researcher would return with new, better crayons. A few minutes later, the researcher came back. To one group of kids he apologized and said he had made a mistake; there were no other crayons. This was the group that experienced an "unreliable" environment. To the other group of kids he gave the new sparkly crayons. This was the group that experienced a "reliable" environment. Then everyone was given the marshmallow test.

The prediction was that the kids who did not get the promised crayons would now, understandably, have low expectations of the experimenter and thus not bother waiting for a second marshmallow. That is exactly what happened. The kids who had experienced the "unreliable" environment waited on average three minutes and two seconds. The kids who had experienced the "reliable" environment waited, on average, a full twelve minutes and two seconds. In other words, the more uncertain the future is perceived to be, the less likely we are to forgo immediate gratification in favor of future bliss.

Immediate Pleasure over Future Pain

This is all well and good, but what does it have to do with our original problem of inducing action? Alas, the difficulty in trying to change people's behavior by warning them of the spread of disease, loss of money, weight gain, academic failure, or global warming is that these are all *uncertain* future sticks. If the ICU staffer does not sanitize their hands, they may risk illness not immediately, but a few days later. If Sam and his team fail to find ways to cut their client's budget, they may lose millions not now, but in a month. These sticks are all in the future; some are far off in the future. And the future, as we all know, is uncertain. Maybe the ICU staff will disregard handwashing but end up fine. Maybe Sam's team will do nothing and the client will decide to remain anyway. The problem lies in the "maybe." It is difficult to make people work for something that may or may not happen. It is too easy to ignore future sticks and convince ourselves that we will be fine even if we continue with our unfavorable habits. This is why a threat of momentous future harm can sometimes be less effective than a minor reward that is immediate and certain. Even if the threat is certain and immediate (like a definite time-out or negative feedback), it may still be less effective than promising an immediate reliable reward, because of the "Go" circuit in the brain, which ties pleasure with action.

Take the largest health insurance company in South Africa, Discovery. Instead of warning of future disease, Discovery launched a reward program that gave clients immediate points every time they purchased fruits and vegetables in the supermarket, visited the gym, or attended a medical screening. The clients could then use the reward points for a range of purchases. The program was highly effective. People engaged in healthier behavior, and as a consequence, the number of hospital visits was reduced. It was a win-win.

Here is a puzzle, though: if threats and warnings have limited impact, why do we frequently use sticks to try to change someone else's behavior? Even with all I now know, I often find myself telling my students that if they do not work harder, they will fail to get a decent job, or warning my daughter that if she does not put on a warm coat, she will catch a cold. What I should be doing is telling my students that if they work harder, they will produce great papers and eventually attain a fantastic job, and my daughter that if she puts on her coat she will feel nice and warm, remain healthy, and therefore be able to attend her friend's birthday party.

No doubt it is difficult to engage in such reframing. This is because our brain automatically hits Fast-Forward. When I notice a student of mine not working as much as he should, my brain rushes ahead to the future and sees him failing to achieve his desired goals. When I spot my daughter stepping outside with only a T-shirt on in mid-December, my brain imagines her with a runny nose and an irritating cough. (Interestingly, it is easier for us to see possible negative outcomes for others than for ourselves, but that is an issue for another discussion.) This is why our immediate reaction is to warn; our brains have visualized devastation, and we share our gloomy foresight. That, however, may be the wrong approach. We should consciously overcome that instinct and instead highlight what needs to be done to make things better; like saying, "wear a coat and you will stay healthy" and "work hard and you will attain a job." There is an additional benefit to this approach: while warnings and threats (such as "Employees must wash their hands") limit people's sense of control, emphasizing what needs to be done to reap rewards increases it. In the next chapter, we will explore the surprising role of control for the influential mind.

4

⟨◦⟩⟨◦⟩

How You Obtain Power by Letting Go (Agency)

The Joy of Agency and the Fear of Losing Control

Imagine a world where fear is rational. In this world, people would scream at the top of their lungs at the mere sight of a cigarette; a heavy-cream phobia and fear of red meat would be commonplace; panic would creep up and down your spine as soon as you entered a moving vehicle. These fears could be justified: smoking, diet, and driving are closely related to the five leading causes of death—heart disease, cancer, chronic lower respiratory diseases, accidents, and stroke.[1] Yet on the list of the most prevalent phobias, which I provide below, you'll find none of these fears.[2]

The majority of people are not alarmed by things that could eventually kill them. Instead, the most common phobia is arachnophobia—the fear of spiders. This despite the fact that "you have a better chance of getting attacked by a shark, surviving, then getting killed by a falling coconut,"* than dying from spider venom. Approximately six people per year die from spider venom in the United States, a nation of 319 million.[3] We fear things that are unlikely to hurt us—spiders, snakes, and heights. Some people experience panic attacks in open spaces or when encountering dogs or lightning. Others fear elevators and flying. In fact, the only justifiable phobia on the top ten list is the fear of germs—mysophobia—which sits at number 8. Two positions below mysophobia you'll find a particularly intriguing phobia: the fear of holes. The number of people who suffer from hole phobia apparently trumps the number who suffer from cancer phobia, which is number 11 on the list, while the fear of death itself sits at number 12.

The Ten Leading Causes of Death

1. Heart disease
2. Cancer
3. Chronic lower respiratory diseases
4. Accidents (unintentional injuries)
5. Stroke (cerebrovascular diseases)
6. Alzheimer's disease
7. Diabetes
8. Influenza and pneumonia
9. Nephritis, nephrotic syndrome, and nephrosis
10. Intentional self-harm (suicide)

The Twelve Most Common Phobias

1. Arachnophobia: the fear of spiders
2. Ophidiophobia: the fear of snakes
3. Acrophobia: the fear of heights

---

* Well, that is, at least, how one member of an online discussion group humorously put it in a forum regarding the matter (Scrap-Lord, http://forum.deviantart.com/devart/general/2226526).

4. Agoraphobia: the fear of open or crowded spaces
5. Cynophobia: the fear of dogs
6. Astraphobia: the fear of thunder or lightning
7. Claustrophobia: the fear of small spaces like elevators, cramped rooms, and other enclosed places
8. Mysophobia: the fear of germs
9. Aerophobia: the fear of flying
10. Trypophobia: the fear of holes
11. Carcinophobia: the fear of cancer
12. Thanatophobia: the fear of death

Fear Versus Fact

We may chuckle at the ridicule of our fears, but for people who suffer from them, these phobias can be devastating. For example, people with agoraphobia are afraid to leave their homes, which would severely impact anyone's quality of life. Individuals with claustrophobia may refuse to get an MRI even if the procedure is essential for diagnosing a medical condition, because they are uncomfortable in the tight space of the scanner. And aerophobia, the fear of flying, can hinder people's careers and relationships.

Take, for instance, film director Joseph McGinty Nichol, known as "McG." McG had directed *Charlie's Angels*, and following the success of that film, he was contracted by Warner Brothers to direct a new Superman picture, which was to be shot in Australia. One thousand employees were Down Under waiting for McG to arrive. Lights and cameras were ready, and it was time for action. McG had spent a year working on the film prior to shooting. Some $20 million had already been invested in the project. Yet on the day McG was supposed to take a private jet to Sydney from California, he found himself paralyzed by fear. He was unable to get on the plane.[4]

His team tried everything to convince him to board the jet. Reassuring statistics were offered: he was more likely to be killed on the way home from the airport in his car than on the long-haul flight to Sydney. In fact, only about 1,000 people die while flying every year (the odds are approximately 1 in 11 million that you will be killed in an airplane crash), compared to 1.24 million who die in ground-traffic accidents (or odds of 1 in 5,000 that you will be killed in a car crash).[5] McG was well aware of these figures, but they did nothing to calm his nerves. He felt safe in his car, not on a plane. Fear is an emotion, and his emotions were not easily tamed by the facts.

Most people assume that aerophobia is a fear of crashing. That fear is heightened by the extended media coverage devoted to every plane that goes down. The vividness of the tragedy on our TV screens makes us believe that airplanes are more dangerous than they really are. That, however, is not the whole story. If it were, perhaps airlines could simply equip people with data that would change their perceptions. But we know that telling people over and over that planes are safer than cars does little to ease their anxiety.

If it is not a miscalculation of risk, why then do so many fear a 747? Some turn to evolution for answers—humans, unlike birds, do not have wings, and they were never meant to fly. If your ancestors ever found themselves in midair, it usually meant they were about to meet their Creator. And so, the story goes, we inherited a fear of flying from our land-bound ancestors. This theory is intuitively appealing. Our modern fear of spiders, snakes, heights, open spaces, and flying could all be leftovers from a time when those things were truly hazardous. In open spaces, for example, you have nowhere to hide from a predator. So those individuals who feared, and thus avoided, open spaces were perhaps more likely to survive. These types of explanations, however, do not capture the full complexity of human fear, because often what we seem to dread is not what we really fear.

Removing Control

"In reality, it was a control issue: Whenever I got outside my comfort zone, I just felt like I was going to die," McG said when trying to explain his refusal to board that dreaded flight to Australia.[6] When you get on a plane, you transfer your destiny, at least for the next few hours, to the pilot and crew. You cannot control the plane's path or its speed. You cannot leave the aircraft at will if you get tired of the crying children or your seatmate's elbow shoving. In fact, the only choice available to you is pretzels or peanuts. Moreover, you have very limited information. You don't know if those bumps you're experiencing are from routine turbulence or something to be concerned about. You don't know if the pilot is tired or alert, or if you're going to arrive on time. The loss of control is a disturbing sensation.

Most people become stressed and anxious when their ability to control their environment is removed. This is why many people prefer sitting in the driver's seat rather than in the passenger's seat, and also why we feel anxious when we are stuck in traffic, unable to move. Limited control is why some dislike being a guest in another's home. It's why physical restraint is psychologically disturbing for humans and animals. Even infants prefer to exercise their limited ability to control their surroundings; once they learn to hold their own bottle, they will express distress when this privilege is taken away. When those infants develop into toddlers, they demand to do everything themselves, from pressing the elevator button to putting on their shoes. Attempts to interfere with their ability to exercise control can lead to tantrums. While adults rarely throw themselves on the floor, banging their hands and feet, when their freedom is taken away, they will feel troubled when their agency is restricted.

The fear of losing control cannot, of course, account for all of our phobias and deep anxieties. Yet, all else being equal, we fear the uncontrollable more than the controllable. Untamed animals, lightning, small spaces that restrict our movements—all of these cause more anxiety than situations that we *perceive* as being under our control, such as cycling, owning a firearm, or medicating ourselves, though these latter activities are, in fact, more dangerous. The attempt to regain control can also contribute to psychological problems, including eating disorders (in which people strictly control what enters their bodies), addiction (which can be an attempt at regulating one's inner state and mood), and even suicide (the decision to end one's life may be viewed as an attempt to control what is typically outside our control).

Empower for Influence

Control is tightly related to influence. When you alter someone's beliefs or actions you are, to some extent, exerting control over that individual. When you are influenced by another, you are giving that individual control over you. This is why understanding the delicate relationship humans have with control is fundamental for understanding influence. It will enable us to better predict when people will resist influence and when they will welcome it.

What we are about to see is that in order to affect another person, we need to overcome our own instinct for control and consider the other's need for agency. This is because when people perceive their own agency as being removed, they resist. Yet if they perceive their agency as being expanded, they embrace the experience and find it rewarding.

A wonderful illustration of this principle involves . . . taxes. Paying taxes makes people unhappy—pure and simple. Even if you agree wholeheartedly that paying taxes is the right thing to do, I am pretty sure you don't feel any pleasure handing over 30 or 20 or even 10 percent of your earnings to the government. In fact, some people decide to avoid the ordeal altogether; the amount of tax evasion in the United States comes to about $458 billion annually.[7] That figure does not even include the amount lost because of people who exploit loopholes. So imagine you are a government official and your task is to reduce that number significantly. Conventional tools for influencing people to pay their taxes already include increasing fines, enhancing audit rates, and highlighting the importance of taxes for the country. Those are useful, but the rate of noncompliance is still high. What else could you do?

Could you, perhaps, make paying taxes more pleasant? This may seem like a radical idea. Let's consider why taxes are so painful in the first place. Yes, by paying taxes we are losing a big chunk of our income, but that is not the sole reason that people find taxes unpleasant. You would probably not feel as much pain if you donated 30 percent of your income to a charity of your choice. The reason paying taxes is more aversive than other expenses is that we have no choice in the matter. In contrast to charity giving or grocery shopping, in which you decide what to pay for and when, spending money on taxes is out of your control. No one asked you if you were willing to pay, and you are not quite certain where your money is going.

Would people be more likely to pay taxes if their sense of agency was recovered? To test this, three researchers conducted an experiment.[8] They invited students to a lab at Harvard University and asked them to rate pictures of various home interiors. In exchange for their time, they were given $10, but told that they were required to pay a "lab tax" of $3. The instruction was to put $3 in an envelope and hand it to the experimenter before they left. The students were not thrilled by this plan. Only half complied; the other half either left the envelope empty or gave less than the required amount.

Another group of participants, however, was told that they could advise the lab manager on how to allocate their tax money. They could suggest, for example, that their taxes would be spent on beverages and snacks for future participants. Astonishingly, merely giving participants a voice increased compliance from about 50 percent to almost 70 percent! That is dramatic. Imagine what such an increase in compliance would mean for your country, if it were translated to federal taxes.

To make sure the finding was not specific to elite Harvard students, the researchers tested a larger, more diverse sample of citizens online. This time some participants were given an opportunity to read about the current allocation of U.S. federal tax dollars. Some were also given an opportunity to express their preferences about how they wanted their tax to be allocated—what percentage they wanted to devote to education, security, health care, and so on. Finally, all of them were asked to imagine that they could use a questionable tax loophole to lower their tax bill by 10 percent—would they take it?

Of those who were not given an opportunity to express their preference on how their taxes should be spent, 2 out of 3 (about 66 percent) said that yes, they would take the questionable loophole. In comparison, among those who were given a voice, less than half (44 percent) decided to take the loophole. The study also revealed that providing people with information about how their money would be spent was not enough. It was giving people a sense of agency that made the difference.

The message, perhaps ironically, is that to influence actions, you need to give people a sense of control. Eliminate the sense of agency and you get anger, frustration, and resistance. Expand people's sense of influence over their world and you increase their motivation and compliance. In the experiments I described, people were not even given actual control—they were only asked to suggest how they would like their taxes to be allocated. Yet that was enough to change their actions. Giving people a choice, even if it is just a hypothetical one, is enough to enhance their sense of control, and control motivates people.

Choosing to Choose

Why do we enjoy control? Well, often outcomes that you select yourself suit your preferences and needs better than those that have been forced upon you. So we have learned that environments in which we can exercise control are more rewarding. One way to express control is to make a choice.[9] For example, if *you* choose which movie to watch, you are more likely (on average) to select a movie you will enjoy than if I make the choice for you. Because we often experience better outcomes following choice, the association between choice and reward has become so strong in our minds that choice itself has become rewarding—something we seek and enjoy. In a study conducted at Rutgers University, neuroscientist Mauricio Delgado and his team found that telling people they were about to be given an opportunity to make a choice made them feel good and activated part of their brain's reward system, the ventral striatum.[10] We perceive choice as a reward in and of itself, and so when given a choice, we choose to choose.[11]

It is not only humans who like to choose; animals prefer to have a choice as well. In fact, they choose to choose even if having a choice does not change the outcome. If rats need to select between two paths that lead to food—one path is a straight line and the other subsequently requires them to select whether to go right or left—they choose the latter path.[12] Pigeons do the same thing.[13] Give a pigeon two options: the first is a button to peck that results in grain being dispensed, and the second is *two* buttons from which it needs to select one to peck in order to receive the same grain, and the bird will pick the option with two buttons. The pigeons quickly learn that the seeds are no different; yet they prefer the seeds that were obtained by making a choice.

As with pigeons and rats, the human desire for agency, control, and choice spills over to situations in which making a choice does not necessarily improve the end result. Take Delgado's experiment, for example. The choice he gave his volunteers was not between banana nut ice cream and mint pistachio, in which a person might have a strong preference, but between two shapes on a computer screen, such as a purple ellipse or a pink star. Each shape had a 50 percent chance of gaining the participant money. As there was no way of knowing which shape was the better shape, it did not matter in the slightest whether the participants made the choice or a computer program made the choice for them. Nevertheless, Delgado's results showed that even when making a choice does not appear to have any advantage, we would often rather take control and decide on our own. This preference is deeply rooted in our biology.

If you think about it, a system that internally "rewards" you for things you obtained yourself, rather than those that were simply given to you, makes adaptive sense. If you learn that an action results in food, money, or prestige, you might choose to repeat that action in the future to gain more of the same. However, if someone simply gives you food, money, or prestige without your having done anything for it, you cannot assume that they will be kind enough to offer you those goods in the future. So when you get $1,000 without doing anything at all, you are left with $1,000 but without any knowledge of how to acquire more money in the future. However, if you gain $1,000 by, for example, selling a piece of furniture, you not only become $1,000 richer, you now have a blueprint of how to earn more money. Things you work for *should* be coded by your brain as preferred; their value comes both from their intrinsic utility *and* from the information they contain for future gains. It is adaptive for humans to be biologically driven to prefer things they had a hand in obtaining—things they have control over.

People like to choose, so they choose to choose.[14] However, sometimes the decision is so complex and taxing that we prefer not to make a decision. For example, if you give people too many options, they become overwhelmed and don't choose anything. This was shown in Sheena Iyengar and Mark Lepper's famous jam study.[15] Iyengar and Lepper found that people are more likely to purchase gourmet jams when they have only six options to choose from versus when they have more than twenty options. Options are great, but give people too many and they become flabbergasted and leave the store empty-handed.

What, then, do you do when you have many options you want people to choose from? One solution may be to create a tree of choice. Let's take the jam problem as an example. Instead of just displaying twenty jams, all together, the store could divide the jams according to flavor: strawberry, apricot, blueberry, marmalade, raspberry. Now the jam buyer only needs to select one flavor out of five. Once they select the flavor—let's say apricot—they can then make a second choice between four different brands. That way people get to make a choice, but the process is simplified.

A Price for Choice

The problem emerges when our desire for control results in otherwise worse outcomes. Take Theo, for example.* Theo is a middle-aged bartender who works at a downtown restaurant in the city of Los Angeles. Every night at the end of his shift, Theo gathers the loose change and bills he earned from tips and stashes the loot under his mattress for safekeeping. Over the years, a significant amount has accumulated under his bedding, such that the clacking of the coins keeps him awake at night. Theo is aware that by hiding the money in his bedroom, rather than depositing it in a savings or investment account, he is losing interest on his earnings. Yet from Theo's perspective, this loss is worth the peace of mind he experiences from feeling he has full control over his funds.

It is for similar reasons that many people hold too much money in cash accounts than is otherwise optimal. When surveyed by a large financial institution, two out of every five respondents said having money in "cash" (such as a checking account) made them feel safe. A similar percentage of respondents said they preferred a cash account because they were risk averse and/or wanted to keep their options open. Investing can make people feel anxious, but the root cause for this is not just risk. The fact that the fate of the investment is not in the individuals' hands, but in the hands of

---

* Theo's identifying details have been altered.

the companies and sectors they are investing in, makes people uncomfortable. When people do invest, they prefer to invest "under their mattress," so to speak—84 percent of respondents said they favored investing domestically, even though the survey was conducted in a part of the world where investing domestically was not necessarily the optimal decision.

To be sure, domestic preference can be driven by patriotic considerations, or by the fact that people may have more information about their own economy than that of others, but the preference is also driven by an illusionary sense that *our domestic* economy is more under our control than a foreign economy. The closer the money, the safer people feel. If you want someone to invest in your company, it may be wise to give them a sense that their investment will remain close—either physically (i.e., in the physical location of your company) or mentally (perhaps your company is within the sector they are most familiar with).

Financial choices are much more emotional than most of us realize. Often the complex reasons for these decisions are hidden from sight. Think back to Theo, the bartender who saved his tips under his mattress. Theo was keeping his money close to his chest, literally, not only because he disliked the idea of transferring it to the hands of others but also because he was trying to guard his earnings from . . . himself. When surveyed about his financial habits, Theo admitted that he kept his money in coins under his old mattress in order to curb his spending impulses. He did not carry the heavy coins around with him in his small wallet, nor did he have a debit card, so if he happened to see a new pair of boots or sunglasses he fancied, he was unable to buy them on the spot. Theo had to go all the way back home, count the coins, and return to the shop to make the purchase. This system gave him ample time to consider his purchase, protecting him from impulse buys. In essence, "present-day Theo" was trying to control "future-day Theo." When it came to money, Theo trusted himself more than he trusted other people, but he also trusted himself today, under a relatively controlled environment, more than tomorrow, when anything might happen.

These days, most people do not keep bills and coins under their mattresses, or diamonds in their bras—a custom that was apparently popular after World War II. Yet the need to personally control our finances remains strong. One of the ways people try to maintain control is with "stock picking." Consider Manshu, who writes the financial blog *OneMint*.[16] Manshu is a self-proclaimed stock picker. This means that instead of hiring a financial adviser to invest for him or putting his money in an index fund, he does his own research and selects the companies whose stocks he wants to buy.

"I like to pick stocks," he explains, "because I prefer to be able to manage my own stocks and know exactly where my money is invested. I don't feel comfortable about buying mutual funds or ETFs [exchange-traded funds] because I don't have any control over what the fund manager may do and which companies he or she will buy at any given time. It's like being one level away from my investments. . . . I worry about what the fund manager would do."[17]

Given that Manshu writes a financial blog, I suspect that he is familiar with the vast research indicating that, on average, investors lose when they pick stocks and trade frequently. In fact, people who choose their own stocks are the worst performers in the market. But even if you let a professional do the job for you, your portfolio will likely underperform index funds and ETFs.[18] Armed with this knowledge, why does Manshu prefer to pick stocks?

You may think Manshu is overconfident. True, overconfidence is a common explanation for why people prefer to make their own choices. They may know the facts and figures but believe *they* can do better than the average guy. Overconfidence does play an important role.[19] Notice, however, that Manshu does not defend his actions by stating that he believes he will make more money by choosing stocks himself. Rather, he justifies his preference in emotional terms: picking his own investments makes him feel in control, while letting someone else choose for him causes him to worry. He prefers "stock picking" to reduce his anxiety and enhance his feeling of mastery, regardless of whether the strategy inflates his bank account. He wants to feel that *he* is influencing his finances, not anyone else.

If there was a psychological cost to giving up control, would people consciously forgo money in order to maintain it? My colleague Cass Sunstein (whom we met earlier), my student Sebastian Bobadilla-Suarez, and I conducted an experiment to find out.[20] We asked volunteers to play a "shape-picking game." In this game, participants were asked to choose between two shapes on a computer screen, only one of which would earn them money. On every trial, two new shapes appeared. We let participants practice the game for a while so that they could get a sense of how good they were at picking the best shapes. Unbeknownst to the participants, we set up the game so that their likelihood of selecting the "winning" shape was exactly 50 percent; they succeeded on half the trials and failed on the other half. After some practice, we asked them to estimate how well they were doing. On the whole, our participants slightly overestimated their ability, stating they believed they were performing above chance. There were large individual differences, however: some people were highly overconfident, believing they could pick the correct shape with 80 percent accuracy, and others were underconfident, believing they could do so only with 20 percent accuracy.

Now that each person had a sense of how good they thought they were at "shape picking," we gave them an opportunity to employ an expert to help them pick the best shapes. Each expert had a different likelihood of picking the better shape and charged a small fee if they were successful in helping the participant make the right choice. For example, some experts picked the best shape 90 percent of the time and charged 10 pence, others did so 75 percent of the time and charged 5 pence, and so on. The success rates and charges were fully visible to the participants, so in essence, with the help of some math, each person could calculate whether it was worthwhile for them to "hire" the expert or not. They had all the information they needed to make the best choices. Would they?

Change the words "shape picking" into "stock picking" and you can see how this game (loosely) resembles real-world financial decisions. Pick on your own, and on average you will do no better than chance. Choose EFTs or index funds, and you can do slightly better than chance, at a low cost. Although our participants sometimes decided to hire an expert "shape picker," they did so less than they should have. We designed the game so that to win the most amounts of money, people should have delegated the decision to an expert on half the trials. Yet our participants delegated the decision to experts only about one-third of the time. They chose to choose, which made them lose. Even if you take into account the participants' overconfidence, people decided to pick for themselves more often than they should have.

The interesting thing was that the participants were aware of what they were doing. When we asked them how good they were at delegating—in other words, did they think they hired experts when they should have—they gave us surprisingly accurate answers. Those who delegated less than they should have knew it; those who delegated optimally also knew it. It seemed that people knew they were losing money by retaining control but did it anyway for psychological gains. Their cost-benefit analysis was not a cold calculation of pennies and dimes but, rather, one that took into account emotional profit.

Of course, in some situations, weighing the costs and benefits of choosing versus delegating may direct us the other way. For instance, even though choosing can give us a small burst of pleasure, we may realize that in certain situations, the benefit of having an expert select for us outweighs the emotional benefit of agency, because the outcome may be that much better. There are other reasons to delegate as well; perhaps you do not have enough time to make the decision, the effort would be too onerous, or you don't want to take responsibility for the outcome. For instance, you might prefer to have your spouse make an important decision concerning your family's future, or for a coworker to make a professional decision for your group so that you can avoid regret if the outcome turns out to be suboptimal. Nevertheless, in all these cases, people still want the power to choose to delegate rather than have that decision forced upon them. It is best, then, to give people that option. For example, I will often ask my three-year-old daughter, "Do you want me to choose your outfit or do you want to choose it yourself?" Sometimes she wants to choose herself, and sometimes she would rather have me choose. Exercising the power of delegation maintains agency.

Control, Health, and Well-Being

People who feel in control of their life are happier and healthier.[21] With that in mind, we can see that the participants in our study, as well as Manshu and Theo, may have been acting "rationally"—by retaining control, they were enhancing their well-being. For example, all else being equal, cancer patients who have a greater perception of control survive longer. Lower risk of cardiovascular disease has also been associated with a greater perception of control.[22] This is not surprising; the sense of control reduces fear, anxiety, and stress—all things that have a detrimental effect on our bodies.

Can we then enhance people's sense of control in order to increase their well-being? In a classic study conducted back in the 1970s, Judith Rodin, from Yale University, and Ellen Langer, from Harvard University, intended to find out.[23] Rodin and Langer were concerned with a specific group of people who had experienced a severe reduction in control. It was an interesting group, because if we are lucky enough, we will eventually become a part of it—the elderly. As we age, we experience a steady decline in our ability to control our lives and our surroundings. For some, this decline begins with retirement and the loss of agency we normally gain from our professional life. It then continues with a deterioration of physical health. The reduction in agency is most pronounced when people move into nursing homes. Suddenly, the decisions you had made for the entirety of your adult life are made for you: your daily schedule, what you eat and when, how you spend your leisure time. Tasks you may have performed yourself—driving, shopping, cooking—are all done for you. It's like being on a plane for the rest of your life. The pilot is full of good intentions, but she is not you.

That is where Rodin and Langer came in. Their idea was to put the elderly back in the pilot's seat. What if the residents of a nursing home were given more choices, more responsibility, and a greater sense of agency? Would they become healthier and happier? In other words, could Rodin and Langer positively influence the life of the elderly by enhancing their sense of control? The two researchers contacted a nursing home in Connecticut and asked the directors whether they would consent to participate in an experiment to find out. They agreed.

The home had residents on four floors, and Rodin and Langer randomly picked one floor to be the "agency" floor and another to be the "no agency" floor. The residents living on the "agency" floor were gathered together and addressed by the staff. They were told that they were expected to take full responsibility for themselves; they should make sure they had everything they needed and should make plans for how they would spend their time. In addition, each resident was given a gift—a potted green plant for their room, which was to be their sole responsibility. The residents on the "no agency" floor were also gathered together. However, in contrast to the "agency" group, they were told that the staff would take wonderful care of them. They did not need to lift a finger. Each resident in this group, too, was given a green plant for their room, but they were told that the staff would water it. There was no real difference in the residents' reality on the two floors; a person living on the "no agency" floor could, if they wanted, water their plant at any time and make as many decisions for themselves as their friend on the "agency" floor could. However, their perception of their own agency was different—and as a result, their actions were different; they were less likely to take control.

Three weeks later, when Rodin and Langer assessed the nursing home residents, they discovered that those individuals who'd been encouraged to take more control over their environment were the happiest and participated in the greatest number of activities. Their mental alertness improved, and eighteen months later they were healthier than the residents on the "no agency" floor.

To me, what is striking about this study, and others like it, is how simple the intervention was. Just giving people a little responsibility, and reminding them that they had a choice, enhanced their well-being. This lesson is extremely valuable for our home life and work life. If you are a parent, you might give your children more responsibilities. At work, employees can be made to have increased involvement in decision-making processes to enhance their motivation and satisfaction. If you are in a relationship, it might help to make sure you are giving your partner a decent say in how you lead your lives as a couple. What is interesting is that the *sense* of control need only be that—a *perception*. It is

Figure 4.1. Agency. *Increase people's sense of control.* *Our instinct when trying to influence others' actions is to give orders. This approach often fails, because when people feel their independence has been limited, they get anxious and demotivated and are likely to retaliate. In contrast, expanding people's sense of agency makes them happier, healthier, more productive, and more compliant. For example, giving people an opportunity to advise how their taxes should be allocated increased the likelihood that they would pay them in full. To produce impact, we often need to overcome our instinct to control and instead offer a choice.*

better to *guide* people toward ultimate solutions while at the same time maintaining their sense of agency, rather than to give orders.

Think back to the story at the beginning of chapter 3—the intervention in the hospital on the East Coast aimed at getting staff members to wash their hands. One of the reasons the intervention was so successful is that instead of using the common approach—a command: "Employees must wash their hands"—the hospital introduced an electronic board that gave the medical staffers positive feedback every time they sanitized their hands. Instead of limiting the staff's sense of agency by giving an order, management expanded it by giving the staffers a feeling that it was their own responsibility to become better. Increasing the perception of control is a cost-efficient way to improve people's personal and professional lives.

Do You Recall Being in Control?

A few years ago, I read an article written by Michael Norton from Harvard Business School. Michael was describing a series of studies he and his colleagues conducted that illustrated a phenomena he called the "IKEA effect."[24] The IKEA effect concerns the observation that people value things they create themselves more than the exact same items created by someone else. For example, if you put together an IKEA shelf yourself, you tend to think it is better than the exact same shelf put together by someone else. In fact, you may think it is better even if you end up with a crooked shelf. Knitted scarves, tree houses, cheese lasagna—if you made it yourself, you usually value it more.

In my view, this was an instance where the *value* of control—in this case, in the form of manipulating objects around us—shone on the objects we created, making them seem better. I wondered, however, whether you actually had to create an item in order to value it more, or whether *believing* you had created an item would be enough for it to shine brighter. So I contacted Michael Norton, and together with my student Raphael Koster and our colleague Ray Dolan, we conducted a study to find out if the perception of control is all we really need to reap the positive benefits of agency.[25]

An incident I'd experienced not long before made me think it might. A few years ago, my parents moved out of my childhood home to a townhouse close to the city. In the process of sorting through the items we had accumulated over the decades, I found a set of paintings I'd made as a teenager. I particularly liked a landscape oil painting and took it to hang in my own home. I got great enjoyment from the painting, which was now on my bedroom wall. I was quite impressed with the ability of my younger self to create such a thing. The picture made me happy. Then one day, while examining the piece of art with shameless self-admiration, I noticed a signature at the corner of the painting. I had missed it before, as it was barely visible. To my surprise, the signature staring back at me was not my own. Someone else's name was printed on my wonderful creation. Within seconds, my perception of the painting changed. Suddenly the strokes seemed too rough, the colors exaggerated, and the subject matter cheesy. Needless to say, the painting came down soon after. It was swiftly replaced with a photo of my kids. At the very least, I could be certain they were my own creation.

I am not implying, of course, that we can't appreciate the creations of others. You need not write a novel, conduct a piece of music, or cook a gourmet dinner to enjoy these things. Nor do we always value our own handmade items more than those of others. However, I pondered whether, all else being equal, *believing* that you created something gave it an extra spark, regardless of whether you had actually made it yourself.

I designed an experiment to test this idea. It involved designing Converse shoes. First, I would invite volunteers into the lab and ask them to evaluate eighty different Converse shoes on a computer screen. Each shoe would be slightly different in color and design. Then, for each volunteer, I would divide all of the shoes into two groups: half the shoes would be assigned to the "create" group and half to the "just watch" group. For the forty "create" shoes, the volunteer would have to log on to the Converse website and use the special online tool there to re-create the exact same shoe. The Converse website used to have an application that allowed anyone to design their own shoe. Notice, however, that the design and colors of the shoes in this experiment were predetermined; the volunteer did not create their favorite design—they simply *re-created* a design we had already made. For the forty "just watch" shoes, I asked my volunteers to watch a video on the computer screen of the shoe being created. They would sit passively in front of the computer watching, rather than clicking buttons themselves. That was the only difference between the "create" shoes and the "just watch" shoes. When the volunteers were done, two hours later, they were asked to evaluate all the shoes again.

Similar to my oil painting saga, the volunteers liked the shoes they thought they had created two hours before better than the ones they remembered "just watching." Which shoes they actually created did not matter at all. The only thing that mattered was which shoes they *believed* they had created. Eighty different shoes are a lot to remember, and so sometimes a volunteer would recall creating a shoe they had "just watched" or recall "just watching" a shoe they had in fact created. The memory of creation, true or false, was enough to make people more appreciative of the shoe. When their memory failed them, the benefits of creation were lost; if someone created a lovely red shoe with blue stripes and green shoelaces but later thought they had "just watched" the shoe being created, they did not value it more.

What this means is that it may not be enough to give people responsibility and choice—they also need to be reminded that they have exercised their control. If Margaret, a lady with silver hair who resided on the "agency floor" of her Connecticut nursing home, had forgotten that she had watered her plant, the nursing staff would be advised to remind her of it, so that she would benefit from exercising her agency. In other words, perception is what matters, not objective reality. To make people value objects more, we need to let them feel that they somehow had a hand in the design.

* * *

We often envision the brain as an organ whose ultimate function is thinking, a sort of biological headquarters for imagination, rumination, and ideas. While it does, of course, execute those functions, those are not your brain's main agenda. The brain has evolved to control our bodies so that our bodies can manipulate our environments.[26] "Govern your surroundings" would be your brain's slogan, if it had one. Our biology is set up so that we are driven to be causal agents; we are internally rewarded with a feeling of satisfaction when we are in control, and internally punished with anxiety when we are not. In general, that is a good piece of engineering; controlling our environment helps us thrive and survive. Yet the price we pay for our intense desire for control is our difficulty to give it up when we should.

At times we should just sit back and enjoy the ride. We should be delighted that the pilot has full control over our plane, not us. If we were in control of the airplane, we would most likely be dead. It is best to allow your doctor, who has years of medical education and hands-on experience, to make medical decisions for you. It is wise to keep your money in a bank, not under your mattress, and to avoid stock picking. But there is nothing more terrifying than giving away control to another human being.

This is why many managers feel the need to micromanage their teams, even if by doing so they are hurting productivity and morale. To produce impact, we often need to overcome our instinct to control and instead offer a choice.

It is difficult to let go, but awareness can help. Understanding why we are the way we are, and being conscious of our deeply rooted drive to make decisions, may help us hand over the wheel once in a while. With awareness comes the understanding that giving away control, even a little, even just the perception of it, is a simple but hugely effective way to increase people's well-being and motivation.[27] Ironically, releasing control is a powerful tool of influence. For example, a parent may want to ask a child who is a picky eater to make their own salad, to enhance the likelihood that they will eat their greens. Students can be offered the opportunity to build their own syllabus in order to increase their interest in their studies. Clients can be encouraged to make more choices, to boost their satisfaction. Employees can help create company rules, to facilitate their own motivation. Promoting self-creation is a great way to help others become happier, healthier, and more successful. Offering control, or even perceived control, is ultimately the best way to get people to act.

⟞⟝⟞

5

What Do People Really Want to Know? (Curiosity)

The Value of Information and the Burden of Knowledge

The next time you are seated in an aircraft that is about to take off, look around yourself during the preflight safety demonstration. How many people are paying attention to the potentially lifesaving instructions? How many are scrolling through Facebook for essential last-minute updates from friends? You would think the passengers would be a captive audience; they are literally stuck in their seats with nowhere to go. Yet a quick look around will confirm that most people would rather entertain themselves than pay attention to the crew.

You may argue that we have all been through the drill before: seat belt, oxygen mask, life jacket, exit door—we get it. But the fact of the matter is that different airplanes have different safety features. In fact, even if you have flown on the exact same aircraft before, you should listen closely. This is because rehearsing the safety procedure just before takeoff reactivates the required sequence in your brain, which makes it more likely that you will execute the actions automatically if needed. In a state of emergency, quick reactions are crucial.

The airline personnel were rightfully concerned that most passengers would not instinctively know to identify their closest exit, or to recall where their life jacket was or how to inflate it safely. They were faced with a difficult problem: they had to ensure that essential information would be transferred from the crew to the passengers, who were simply not interested in paying attention.

The difficulty was that the message the crew had to convey did not seem new or useful. What's more, people did not want to think about emergency landings, fires, or lack of oxygen just before takeoff. Checking the weather or looking at yet another baby photo on Facebook provides more pleasant data for your mind. For years, the airlines tried to find a solution. How could they make people pay attention to this important but unpleasant, information? How could they captivate the passengers and influence their actions? And then it dawned on them. There was no need for the message to evoke dread. People want sunshine? They will give them sunshine!

Preflight safety demonstration videos now include everything from models break-dancing in bathing suits to cute cartoons and stand-up comedy. Many highlight enchanting travel destinations. And people watch them, because they fulfill at least one of the principles that make people want to pay attention: they induce positive emotions.

In fact, the videos are so popular that people even view them at home. One of Virgin America's preflight safety videos that includes music and dancing received 5.8 million YouTube views, 430,000 Facebook shares, and 17,000 tweets in only twelve days.[1]

There is a vital lesson here. Whether at work or at home, our instinct is that if we have something important to convey, the other person will want to know. This instinct is wrong. If people do not even pay attention to information that could potentially save their lives, you cannot presume they will hear what you have to say. We need to rethink what really causes people to want to listen and then reframe our message accordingly, because being heard is by far the most important ingredient for influence. What, then, do people want to know?

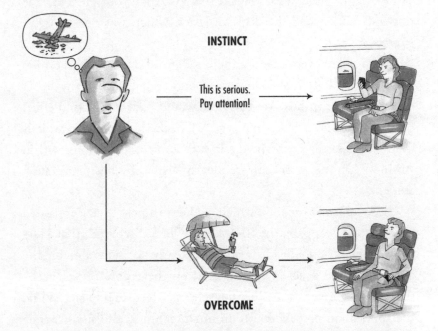

Figure 5.1. Curiosity. *Reframe the message to highlight the possibility for progress, rather than doom. Our intuition is that if we have something important to convey, others will want to know it. This instinct is wrong. In particular, if the information is tied to a bleak message, many will actively avoid it—as was the case with preflight safety briefings. Reframe your message so that the information you provide will induce positive feelings (as the airlines did), highlight the informational gap you are filling, and show how the knowledge can be used for the better.*

Fill the Gap

In 2005, Kate, an investment banker with a large firm in Manhattan, decided to apply to business school for an MBA. Her top choice was Harvard. She invested a substantial amount of time and effort in her application, studying day and night for the Graduate Management Admission Test (GMAT), taking pains to craft an impressive personal statement, and making sure her references were impressive.* Before the deadline arrived, she submitted her application on the designated website—www.ApplyYourself.com. She restlessly anticipated the decision letter, which was due to arrive March 30.

Then, a few weeks before the big date, she received an e-mail from a friend. It looked innocent enough, just like any other message in her in-box. Yet this note would have a profound effect on her life. The subject line read, "Check this out—the wait is over!" The message contained a link to a forum discussion within Business Online, a website frequently visited by business school students.

Kate followed the link, which led her to a post by a user named "Brookbond." Apparently, "Brookbond" had discovered that Harvard Business School had already made early decisions about many applicants. The decisions were stored on the ApplyYourself website, which Harvard and other top schools were using to streamline the application process. With minimal technical skills, any applicant could view their decision letter early. "Brookbond" went on to post detailed instructions on how to do so. All that was required was that Kate log on to the ApplyYourself website with her known

---

* Credit to Ethan Bromberg-Martin, who drew my attention to this story during a conversation. Kate is a fictitious prototype of the 119 students involved in the actual event, which occurred in 2005.

ID and password, just as she had done many times before. Once she was logged on, she was to construct a special URL, the details of which "Brookbond" had supplied. Then she would view either a rejection letter or a blank screen. The latter indicated acceptance to Harvard Business School.

Instinctively, Kate opened a new browser and, with shaking hands, typed in the website's address. Her heart pounding, she logged on and constructed the special URL, closely following Brookbond's instructions. She took a deep breath and hit "Enter." It seemed like forever, but a split second later, the browser refreshed and—nothing. A blank page! It was the most beautiful, inspiring blank page she had ever seen. Kate was thrilled—she was heading to Harvard Business School.

Except she wasn't. Around midnight that same day, senior members of the Harvard admissions department would receive a call from one of the applicants alerting them to the system's failure. Immediately, a team of experts was designated to solve the problem, and by nine o'clock the next morning the bug had been fixed. Shortly afterward, Harvard would announce the rejection of all 119 applicants who attempted to get a sneak peek. As far as Harvard was concerned, the act was a breach of ethics.[2]

I don't know about you, but I can identify with Kate. I clearly remember, years ago, anxiously waiting to hear whether I'd gotten into graduate school. I was restless for months, and during those last few weeks before admission day, I could hardly sleep. Thankfully, I did not encounter a "Brookbond" sort of character back then. If I had, I hope my younger self would have made a different decision than Kate did. Yet I am certain of one thing: I had a burning desire to know immediately. But why did I want to know so badly? What was driving this urge?

For me, learning the decision early would have had no concrete benefits. I could not change the decision; I did not have any other offers I needed to reply to; it was too late to apply to additional schools; I could keep the job I had if I did not get into a PhD program, so there was no need to seek alternative career plans immediately; I was already living in the same city as the schools I had applied to. In sum, there was no tangible gain for advance information. Yet I really, really, really wanted to know. If I could have legally paid for such (seemingly) useless information, I would have.

The desire to know is human. Walk into your nearest pharmacy, and on the shelves you will find popular devices that offer customers advance looks into their future for as little as ten dollars. These small devices enable certain individuals to learn what their future holds days before reality unfolds. For a little bit extra, you can even purchase top-of-the-line products that will provide the same information as the standard brand twenty-four hours earlier.[3]

If you happen to carry two X chromosomes, you may have guessed what I am referring to: a pregnancy test. While we can make the case for the practical advantage of knowing whether you or your partner is pregnant before it becomes apparent to all, it would be difficult to "rationally" justify spending more money for the opportunity to receive the test result one day earlier.[4] Yet millions of people around the world do exactly that. One reason they do so is to reduce the unpleasant feeling of uncertainty. Even if people cannot use the information to their advantage, they have a desire to fill gaps in their knowledge. Information gaps make people feel uncomfortable, while filling them is satisfying. This is why early pregnancy tests are so popular and why Kate's curiosity got the better of her.

If you possess information that can fill existing gaps in people's knowledge, remind them of those gaps. The e-mail Kate received, for example, with its subject line "Check this out—the wait is over!," did just that. It focused her attention on the fact that she did not know if she would be heading to Harvard come fall. Or consider online clickbait such as "The ten celebrities you never knew were enthusiastic gardeners" or "The three politicians you never knew got a nose job." Those create gaps of knowledge in people's mind that were not there to begin with. I never considered which celebrity adores plants or which politician used to have a crooked nose, but now that this gap of knowledge had been pointed out to me, I have an urge to fill it. Once we are told what we do not know, we want to know. As we are about to discover, the drive is evolutionarily ancient.

Is Information Like Sex and Plum Pie?

In a creative experiment, neuroscientists Ethan Bromberg-Martin and Okihide Hikosaka showed that monkeys, too, prefer to be in the know.[5] The hairy animals were not applying to Harvard Business School, of course; nor were they curious to receive information regarding their reproductive system. What was occupying the monkeys' minds was whether they were about to receive 0.88 milliliters of water (a big reward) or just 0.04 milliliters of water (a small reward).

This is how the experiment worked: on each trial, the monkey would receive either a big water reward or a small water reward. By moving its eyes to one of two symbols on a screen (let's say a blue star or pink square) seconds before the water was delivered, the monkey could indicate if it desired advance information. The monkeys were trained for weeks to make sure they understood what every symbol meant. If the monkey selected to receive this advance information, a third symbol appeared on the screen (for example, a red circle), indicating whether the monkey was about to get lots of water or just a little. Finally, the water was delivered straight into the monkey's dry mouth.

When all the data had been gathered, Bromberg-Martin and Hikosaka were amazed to find that not only did monkeys want advance information, they were also willing to "pay" for it. The monkeys were willing to give up a few drops of precious water in order to know ahead of time if they were about to get a large reward or just a small one. Time and time again, the monkeys would move their eyes to indicate that they wanted to know. It seems that, just like Kate, they, too, would have followed the instructions provided by "Brookbond" and logged on to ApplyYourself.com to get a sneak peek. Human preference for information is thus not unique. In evolutionary terms, it is an ancient desire. What, biologically speaking, is driving the urge?

Bromberg-Martin recorded activity from neurons in the monkeys' brains to find possible answers. He inserted thin wires, called microelectrodes, through the scalp of the monkey, deep into the monkey's brain. The tips were placed next to the neurons he wanted to record from. When neurons "fire," they generate a signal, which flows down the neuron as a current, in and out of the cell. The microelectrode can pick up on these changes in voltage. What Bromberg-Martin observed was that the monkey's brain was treating information as if it was a reward in and of itself. These neurons, known as "dopaminergic neurons," were firing in response to information as they would in response to water or food.

Dopaminergic neurons are cells in the brain that release the neurotransmitter dopamine. These neurons send signals from the midbrain, an evolutionarily "old" part of the brain, to many other regions of the brain, including the striatum, a part of the brain that processes rewards, as well as areas in the front of the brain that are important for planning. Dopamine is released when we expect a reward and when we receive an unexpected reward. Well, it turns out that dopamine is also released when we expect information and when we unexpectedly receive information. In the brain, the "currency" for tangible goodies, like sex and plum pie, looked a lot like the "currency" for pure knowledge. In fact, Bromberg-Martin was stunned to see that the neurons were firing at a similar rate to the expectancy of information as they would to the delivery of 0.17 milliliters of water. In other words, the neurons were as excited by advance knowledge as they were by drops of H_2O, which are necessary for our existence.

These findings may partially explain our obsession with Google and Twitter: we are driven to seek information by the same neural principles that drive us to seek water, nourishment, and sex. Yet the question still remains: why? Why would the human brain code for knowledge as it does for those things that are necessary for survival?

The simple answer is that, in many cases, information is indeed necessary for survival, because advance knowledge can help us make better decisions. In the wild, if the monkey knows it is about to receive a large banana, he can decide to stick around, but if he learns that the banana is small, he may decide to look elsewhere. Granted, in Bromberg-Martin's experiments, the monkeys could not use the information in any useful way—they were stuck in their chairs, and there was nowhere for them to go. But their brains still responded according to the "all-purpose rule" that information is better than ignorance, and almost as important as H_2O.

The Feel-Good Factor

There was another reason that Bromberg-Martin's monkeys wanted to know in advance whether they would be receiving a large gulp of water. Knowing that water was about to arrive made the monkeys feel good, and so they sought out the buzz. What you know affects not only what you decide to *do* but also how you *feel*. This is because information is the bread and butter of your beliefs, and what you believe has a profound effect on how happy you are.

Imagine Oscar and Albert. Albert is in prison. His cell is small, wet, and cold. The walls are bare, and he is wide awake late at night on an uncomfortable wooden bed. You may expect Albert to be miserable, but in fact he is exhilarated, elated. Albert knows that tomorrow he will be released from prison and free to go home. His family is preparing a lovely roast turkey dinner for him, which they will enjoy in their cozy, warm house. He can't wait.

Oscar, on the other hand, is sitting at the dining table with his family, having a delicious roast turkey dinner in their warm and cozy home. You might expect Oscar to be joyful, elated, but in fact his heart is heavy. He is miserable because he knows that tomorrow he will be imprisoned. He will be put in a small, cold, wet cell with bare walls and an uncomfortable wooden bed.

If you were observing Oscar and Albert from afar, ignorant of what is going on inside their heads, you would think that warm, dry, satiated Oscar is happier than cold, wet, hungry Albert. Albert's reality is not one any of us would wish upon ourselves, but inside his mind there is a celebration: balloons are floating, the sun is shining, flowers are blooming. For Albert, knowledge is bliss, salvation from the darkness around him. While Oscar's momentary reality is vastly better than Albert's, what goes on inside his mind is far worse. Knowing that the very next day he will be incarcerated gravely affects his well-being. If Oscar were oblivious to what awaits him, he would feel fine, but he knows, and that knowledge is devastating.

It is important to remember, then, that people are motivated not only to gain rewards and to avoid pain but also to *believe* that they will gain rewards and avoid pain. This is because beliefs can make people as happy or sad as the real events can. Armed with a lifelong experience of being both devastated and elated by knowledge, we have learned that information affects our feelings and that we can use information to regulate our emotions. As a result, people selectively try to fill their minds with knowledge that will form pleasing beliefs and avoid information that can cause unpleasant thoughts. This is one reason that the new preflight announcements did so much better at captivating people's minds.

In one experiment, Filip Gesiarz and I invited people to play a lottery game. Every time they played the game, they were presented with two digital doors—a blue door and a red door. Behind each door awaited a cash prize; some prizes were relatively big, and some were small. The red door was always better than the blue door—behind the shiny red door lay more cash than behind the blue door. A computer program would select one of the doors for the participant at random, and they would be given whatever was behind it. Before the computer made the choice, we allowed people to have a sneak peek behind one door. Would they like to see what was hidden behind the red (large prize) door or the blue (small prize) door? Their decision would have no effect on the outcome. Time and time again, people preferred to open the red door over the blue door. They wanted to know what the best-case scenario was, not the worst.

Does this mean that information is not created equal? Perhaps our brains code for the value of information differently, depending on whether we expect the information to make us feel happy or sad. To answer this question, Caroline Charpentier and I teamed up with Ethan Bromberg-Martin. This time, instead of recording the activity of neurons in a monkey's brain, we recorded activity in the human brain using a brain-imaging scanner.

Imagine you are a participant in our experiment. You meet Caroline, the French experimenter, who explains that you will be lying in a long tube-shaped brain-imaging scanner while playing a lottery game. The game will be divided into two parts. Half of the game will be all about winning. Each time you play the lottery, you will either win one dollar or get nothing. Pretty good, you think. The other half of the game is all about losing. Each time you play the lottery, you will either lose one dollar or lose nothing. Not great, I know, but you have no choice; if you want to participate in the experiment, you must play the game. Oh, and every time you play the lottery, Caroline will ask you if you want to know the outcome of that round of the game or remain ignorant. At the end of the experiment, we will pay you the total of what you earned throughout, regardless of which outcomes you selected to reveal and which to remain ignorant of. Think about it as if you are sitting in front of a slot machine: you close your eyes and pull the lever; the reels spin round and round and eventually stop. Do you open your eyes? Do you want to know?

Just like Kate and Bromberg-Martin's monkeys, people wanted to know. But they wanted to know more about potential wins than potential losses. In other words, people were more likely to open their eyes if they were playing the win-or-nothing slot machine than the lose-or-nothing slot machine. What's more, the better the odds of winning with the slot machine, the more people wanted to know the outcome. We displayed the probability of winning each time people played our little lottery—the more likely people were to win, the more they wanted to know, and the more likely they were to lose, the less they wanted to know. In other words, people want to tear open envelopes that promise good news and toss away ones that promise bad news.

What about the brain? Remember those neurons Bromberg-Martin discovered firing in the monkeys' brains in response to advance information about water? We found evidence that suggested that neurons in the same region in the human brain also increase activation in anticipation of information about financial gains. However, in anticipation of information about losses activation was decreased. In addition, whenever our participants knew information was coming—regardless of whether it was information about losses or wins—another region in the brain, the orbital frontal cortex, was activated. It seems that in our brains there are two types of responses to information; one type of neurons values knowledge per se, and the other type values knowledge that is likely to make us feel good.

Not all information is like sex and plum pie; what people expect to find behind the door matters. People prefer to learn of information that they think will make them feel good, and so they seek out good news over bad news. Transmitting a message in a positive light—as the airlines eventually did with their musical safety information videos—means that people will be more likely to listen and, therefore, more likely to be influenced. When people suspect that bad news is coming, they may *avoid* the message—even if this ignorance can hurt them.

Burying One's Head in the Sand

Envision that you have a 50 percent chance of inheriting a fatal disease. The symptoms of the illness are devastating; they include excruciating changes to your personality, as well as declines in your cognitive and physical skills. You will begin to execute unwanted jerky movements, your speech will become incomprehensible, your sleep will be disturbed, and you are likely to develop depression and anxiety. The disease is not contagious, yet there is no cure, and within twenty years you will be dead. There is a simple test you can take at any time that will tell you whether you are carrying the dreaded gene that causes the disease. If you are, the likelihood of you developing the illness will be 100 percent. You are left with the decision of whether to get tested or to go on with life and hope for the best.

For some people, the question is not hypothetical. These are individuals with a parent who is a known carrier of a mutation to gene *IT15*, which causes Huntington's disease. Huntington's disease is a neurodegenerative genetic disorder. The fatal symptoms usually become apparent in midlife, impairing cognitive and motor function, and lead to severe behavioral, mental, and physical problems. Genetic testing now enables people at risk to know, at any point, whether they are carriers.[6]

The decision to get tested is a difficult one. When potential carriers are asked if they intend to take the test, between 45 and 70 percent say yes. Yet most of them do not follow up on their explicitly stated intention. In fact, one study reported that when approached by the registries of testing centers, only 10 to 20 percent of people at risk for Huntington's choose to register for the test. [7]

Similar behavior has been observed with people at risk of contracting HIV: many avoid being tested for the virus even when the test is offered for free.[8] An even more striking example comes from a study of 396 women who gave a blood sample and were later told that those samples had been analyzed to identify genes that predispose a woman to breast cancer.[9] Would they like to receive the results of the test? The women simply had to say yes, with no effort required. Yet 169 chose not to know. This is quite staggering! Unlike people at risk of developing Huntington's disease, individuals at risk of suffering from breast cancer can take precautionary actions to reduce the likelihood of their developing the disease. Nevertheless, 42 percent of the individuals tested decided not to receive information that could possibly save their lives.

This may seem surprising, but think about it like this: while the benefit of knowing would be to reduce the uncomfortable feeling of uncertainty, the cost of knowledge would be not having the option to believe what you would like to believe. As long as we are ignorant of the test results, we can continue believing that we are healthy; we can fill our minds with positive thoughts. Taking the test puts those thoughts in danger, because once we receive the test results, we cannot unlearn them. Once you know that you carry an ill-fated gene, that knowledge will be engraved in your brain forever. If the diagnosis is undesirable, your life will change instantly. So not knowing can, perhaps, keep us happier at times, but it also has the potential to lead to a worse outcome.

Summing Up the Numbers

Metaphorically speaking, you can think of the decision to know or remain ignorant as an exercise in mental arithmetic. Imagine a powerful calculator with a large display residing inside your head. When you need to decide whether to remain in the dark or find out the truth, it lights up and computes the value of the different options. First, your mental calculator figures out the tangible benefits of finding out the truth—will knowing change your actions in a way that will better your future? Inserting large values here will make it more likely that you will seek concrete answers. For example, let's say you are thinking of Googling an old flame. How would you use that information? Maybe you intend to contact the person to rekindle a friendship. In that case, the value of information will go up. However, if the knowledge is not going to influence your actions, the value assigned here will be zero.

Next, your mental calculator will punch in values to indicate the influence of the state of uncertainty on your emotions. In many cases, uncertainty is experienced negatively, so negative values will be entered. The greater the suffering you are likely to experience from not knowing, the more motivated you will be to resolve the uncertainty and find out the truth. Yet not knowing can have a positive effect, too, since it enables you to imagine the best-case scenario. During those months before Kate received the final decision from Harvard Business School, she excitedly imagined all the great experiences she would have at the school, including the people she would meet and the classes she would take. She fantasized about life with an MBA from Harvard, all the doors that would open up after she earned her degree. Creating those scenarios in her mind made her happy, and as long as she had yet to be rejected, she could go back to those images in her mind anytime she wished.

The last calculation to be made is related to the emotional value of the information itself. Becoming aware of something that we were ignorant of before not only makes us more knowledgeable, it changes how we feel. This is especially true for information that enlightens us about ourselves. Knowing that she had been accepted to Harvard made Kate feel good. Hearing that she'd been rejected for having a sneak peek made her feel terrible. Finding out that you carry a fatal gene will make you feel bad. Reading your boss's glowing report of your work makes you feel proud. Being told that the value of your house is descending makes you anxious. Information changes how you feel.

So *all else being equal*, we seek information that we think will bring us positive emotions. We will go to great lengths to uncover good news and avoid bad news.

One of the most striking examples of this tendency is illustrated in a study conducted by Niklas Karlsson, an expert in business information management in Sweden; George Loewenstein, a renowned behavioral economist from Carnegie Mellon; and Duane Seppi, a professor of financial economics at Carnegie Mellon.[10] The three wanted to know what causes people to check up on their stocks when they have no intention of making a transaction. Take a guess: what triggers people to have a quick peek at the value of their stocks? Assuming that a person has no intention of buying or selling, when do you think they are most likely to log on to their accounts?

Now take a look at figure 5.2 (on next page) and let me walk you through the data. The black line shows the value of the S&P 500 for over a little more than two years, from January 2006 to April 2008. The S&P 500 is a stock market index; it is based on five hundred leading companies with stock on the NASDAQ and/or NYSE. Like an ocean wave, the line gathers momentum, slowly rising and then quickly falling, rising again and falling once more. The gray line represents the number of times people logged on to their accounts just to check on the value of their stocks—not to sell or buy, only to have a peek.* What becomes immediately apparent is that the two lines rise and fall together, like two lovers holding hands on a hike up and down a hill. When the market is high, people log in all the time. When the market is low, they avoid checking their funds. Why?

---

* If you are familiar with the S&P 500, you will notice that this graph shows not the raw numbers but, rather, values that have been controlled for all the obvious confounding factors, including willingness to transact and market volume.

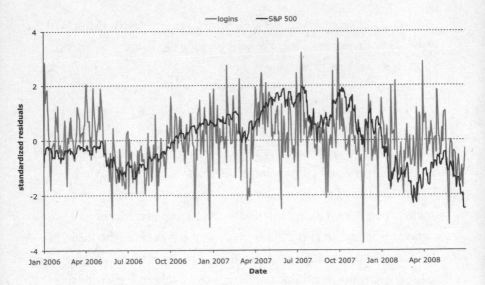

Figure 5.2. *People's desire to know their own worth is related to market performance. The black line represents the S&P 500, and the gray line represents the number of times people logged on to their accounts to check on their stocks. When the market goes up, people are more likely to take a peek at the value of their holdings than when it goes down.*[11]

After statistically accounting for many different factors and possible explanations, the team reached a conclusion: people's decision to gather information about the value of their stocks is governed by their desire to feel good. If the market is heading up, people assume that their own stocks will follow suit, and so they log on to take in a large sniff of the good news. When the market is dropping, they choose to shove their craniums in the ground. People know that there is a chance that they may be losing money, and confirming this will make them feel rotten. If they remain ignorant, they can hold on to some hope that their portfolio is, in fact, weathering the storm. So all else being equal, people tend to ignore negative information, which can make them feel bad, and seek positive news, which can make them feel good.

That, however, is true as long as the bad news can reasonably be ignored. What the graph does not show is what happened when the market finally collapsed, in the fall of 2008. During the financial collapse, people started logging in frantically. When things are very clearly going wrong, keeping a sliver of hope is virtually impossible, and so we set out to assess the damage as soon as we can and rebuild.

This principle does not just apply to finance. While most people at risk of Huntington's disease avoid genetic testing, many of those who decide to take the test are individuals who are already experiencing symptoms. In essence, they are simply confirming what they already know to be true with near certainty. Although the disease cannot be cured, the knowledge can help them make decisions regarding how to live their remaining years. Individuals who know they have a short life span "fast-forward" their lives; they may get married, they may get pregnant, they may retire early.[12] In other words, people select to avoid potentially unwelcome information unless they are almost certain of the devastating news. At that point, the cost of making wrong decisions outweighs the benefit of not knowing how bad things really are.

The Cost of Not Knowing

We may put our heads in the sand in order to shield ourselves from the inconvenient truth, but does it work? Is our mental state actually improved by not knowing? Or perhaps we might fare better by facing the truth?

In 1972 two psychologists, James Averill and Miriam Rosenn, set out to investigate this question in their laboratory at UC Berkeley.[13] They randomly selected male undergraduates from the university's phone directory and rang them with an offer: would they be willing to serve as participants in a study that involved receiving electric shocks in exchange for two dollars an hour? (Which works out to about eleven dollars an hour today.) James and Miriam convinced eighty students to agree to this arrangement.

On the day of the experiment, the men arrived at the Berkeley lab. Each one was asked to sit on a wooden chair while the researcher vigorously rubbed their right ankle with a mildly abrasive paste to lower the skin's resistance. Then an aluminum electrode was attached to their ankle. Every so often, the electrode would generate a shock lasting one second.

The men were given headphones that enabled them to listen to one of two channels, which they could switch between at will. One channel played music via a stereophonic tape recorder from Muzak recordings (remember, this was back in 1972). The other channel was the "information" channel; it was silent except for a clear warning signal a few seconds before a shock was delivered. When the warning signal sounded, the participant could immediately press a button in order to avoid the shock altogether.

The question was which channel would the men select to listen to—the music channel or the information channel? You would think everyone would choose to tune into the information channel to avoid the shocks, wouldn't you? Indeed, an important factor that drives people to seek information is usefulness. When people believe they can use the information you are offering to their benefit, they desire it more, which is why it is important to highlight the usefulness of any message.

Yet in Averill and Rosenn's experiment, although the volunteers could use the information to avoid the shocks, not everyone selected the information channel. Approximately one out of every four men (25 percent) decided to avoid the information channel altogether. They chose to distract themselves with the music, even if it meant receiving electric shocks directly to their skin.

Perhaps this was the better choice? Maybe the music had a relaxing effect? Averill and Rosenn monitored the men's physiological signs to find out. They measured heart rate, skin conductance, and respiratory rate. The more anxious you are, the faster your heart will pound, the more your palms will sweat, and the heavier your breathing will become. Averill and Rosenn found that the men who decided to listen to the music channel expressed *greater* signs of anxiety than those who listened to the information channel. Those who decided to watch out for warnings were more relaxed, because they knew they could avoid harm, and so they ended up feeling better. On the other hand, those who were trying to put their minds in a musical cloud did not succeed in escaping the anxiety brought about by the anticipated pain. The bottom line was that knowing when a shock was coming and being able to control it was better than remaining ignorant.

What if the shocks were unavoidable? Would choosing the information channel benefit people even when the information was otherwise useless? Averill and Rosenn conducted their experiment again, only this time they did not give the Berkeley men a button to enable them to escape the shocks. Under these conditions, most men selected the music channel, but 45 percent of them still selected the information channel. Who ended up more anxious? Once again, those who chose to hide in a musical cloud exhibited greater physiological signs of anxiety. In contrast, the men who selected the information channel were more relaxed; their heart rates were lower, and they sweated less. While they could not avoid the shocks, knowing exactly when one would be delivered enabled them to relax during the breaks in between. In contrast, those who selected the music channel were in a constant state of high alert; they sat on the edge of their seats, ready for the buzzing pain of the shock at any point.

What this experiment shows us is that even if you think you will be better off not knowing, putting your head in the sand may end up making you *more* anxious. To be clear, I am not suggesting that we should all go searching for bad news—not at all! At times, true ignorance can indeed be bliss. It may not be advisable to stalk an ex on social media to learn about their life without you; nor do you need to be aware of every single genetic mutation you carry. But if you suspect that there is uncomfortable news behind door number 1, you may be better off opening it to reveal the truth. This is because we humans are much more resilient than we think. By opening the door we can start the process of acceptance, healing, and rebuilding. If the door remains shut we are stuck, lingering in a constant state of unease.

Cherry-Picking

We are curious creatures, and the one topic we are especially curious about is ourselves. Indeed, we have a burning need to know what other people think of us and our work, but we do not want to know everything. We often make decisions to distance ourselves from negative opinions and seek positive ones. How many times have you heard authors, actors, and celebrities say they avoid Googling themselves or reading reviews about their book/show/ film? Do you think this is because people do not want to learn that their work has been praised? Unlikely.

Take Paige Weaver, for example, who wrote a number of self-published best sellers. Paige says that "my policy is do not read your reviews. . . . The first few days after *Promise Me Darkness* [her novel] was released, I read all the reviews and they were good but I knew that the bad ones were coming. . . . I'm too scared."[14]

Novelist Kristin Cashore agrees. "I have not Googled myself or my books, and I do not get Google alerts. . . . I don't involve myself. I've learned it's better for my writing process, my sanity, and my happiness to avoid it. Besides, I get a ton of feedback without looking for it—my friends and publishers are on the ball and keep me informed of what people are saying—so I generally have a sense of what's going on out there without seeking it out myself. I do usually (though not always) read reviews if my editor or publicity department sends them to me. Those ones tend to be the ones in major review journals, and are hard to ignore."[15]

Paige and Kristin are not unique in cherry-picking the opinions they will become aware of. It is not that we always ignore criticism; our methods are subtler than that. Our decision whether to seek opinions depends both on whether we can use the knowledge to our advantage and on how we expect to feel in response. Nevertheless, we all engage in some filtering. Take Republican ex–vice president Dick Cheney, for example. Before entering a hotel suite, he requests that all TVs be tuned to Fox News, a corporation well known for supporting the Republican Party.[16]

* * *

People at risk of disease who choose not to get tested and students who decide to listen to music over warnings that could help them avoid electric shocks demonstrate the same principle. All else being equal, people have a tendency to seek out information that brings them hope and to avoid information that brings devastation. This is because information affects what people believe, and what people believe affects their well-being. If the information you have to offer is tied to a bleak message, you must assume many will choose to avoid it. You can spend years figuring out the best safety procedures, decades developing a test to identify a gene that puts people at risk of breast cancer, and weeks reviewing a colleague's report. But it doesn't matter how thorough your work is or how clearly you present it if no one wants to know what it says. Perhaps you can do something about this?

Getting people to listen means shifting that large metaphoric calculator inside their minds, the one that computes the value of information and motivates them to pay attention when it shows positive numbers. If the knowledge you have can fill another's information gap, highlight the gap; if it can help people better their world, clarify how. Finally, reframe your message so that the information you provide will induce hope, not dread. To be clear, this does *not* mean sugarcoating what you have to say. If, for example, you need to critique someone's work, do not soften the critique—convey the problem clearly. However, the existing problem can be communicated either in terms of what needs to be corrected in order to produce a star report or in terms of incompetence; use the first approach and you will gain more interest. Perhaps a genetic screening for breast cancer can become all about living a long and healthy life, not about death. And a flight safety video can spotlight arriving at our fabulously sunny destination.

There is an important caveat to all this, though. It is that we need to consider the emotional state of the person in front of us. This is because, as we will see in the next chapter, under stress and intimidation, the way in which our brains process information changes dramatically.

6

⋖⋗

What Happens to Minds
Under Threat? (State)

The Influence of Stress and the Ability to Overcome

When I was a teenager, my favorite TV show was *Quantum Leap*. My brother and I would return home from school in the afternoon just in time to watch physicist Sam Beckett travel through space and time in an attempt to correct history. His quantum experiments enabled him to leap from his top secret laboratory in the desert, somewhere in the United States in the 1990s, into the bodies of individuals living in different places and times.

I invite you to leap with me through space and time to help us understand how stress affects the way people are influenced by others. Our first stop will be New York City on September 14, 2001. The body you will be inhabiting is my own.

I was walking along Broadway in downtown Manhattan, not far from where I lived at the time. Suddenly a middle-aged man began running down the street, seemingly in panic. Within seconds others followed, and within minutes a crowd was sprinting behind him. I had no idea what was going on. Yet the events that had occurred just three days earlier—on September 11, 2011—had taken their toll. "Better safe than sorry," I figured, and joined everyone else. A large group of us ran down the sidewalk, picking up confused bystanders on our way. Eventually a few individuals realized there was nothing to flee and stopped, and shortly after, everyone else did the same. That was that. We all went on with our business.

If you think about it, it was quite extraordinary: one individual caused approximately fifty New Yorkers to stop whatever they were doing and start running, in the middle of the day and for no apparent reason. That person did not say a word; he simply ran down the street in a panic. I do not know what was going on inside *his* head. But the reason he was able to influence us all was because of what was already going on inside *ours*. If the incident had taken place on September 10, the day before the attacks on the World Trade Center, I suspect the sprinting guy would have gone unnoticed. Most of us would have written him off as an eccentric. Yet following the terrorist attacks, we were all on edge. What would happen next? Was another assault imminent? Where would it be coming from? Our minds were on "standby"—ready to react to anyone and anything.

Cue in our next leap, into the body of a seventeen-year-old Palestinian girl in the West Bank village of Arrabah on the morning of March 21, 1983. The girl was sitting in her classroom when suddenly she began experiencing an irritating cough and shortness of breath. She did not know it at the time, but she was about to trigger an international scandal.

Shortly after the girl first began to experience these signs, seven of her classmates fell ill, too; then students in other classrooms began experiencing similar symptoms. A week later, the "condition" had spread to nearby villages. In total, the epidemic affected 943 Palestine girls and a few Israeli soldiers.[1] What was causing this terrible epidemic? The Palestinians accused the Israelis of using chemical weapons against them, while the Israelis accused the Palestinians of using poison to trigger mass demonstrations. Careful investigation, however, did not reveal foul play. The symptoms were diagnosed as psychosomatic. Such cases are sometimes referred to as "mass hysteria"—an individual's symptoms (or behavior) elicit panic among others, who unconsciously adopt the symptoms, thereby activating a domino effect.

Without even intending to, one girl influenced the health of almost one thousand individuals and, eventually, the world. The reason she had such impact was the specific environment she was operating in—one that induced a particular state of mind in others.

What was common to the people fleeing from absolutely nothing in post-9/11 Manhattan and to the students in the West Bank experiencing illusionary illness was that they were operating under threat. The students' reality in the West Bank consisted of missiles, curfews, and armed soldiers on a daily basis. In New York after 9/11, soldiers and policemen were visible everywhere on the streets, creating a sense of emergency. If you look back at the history of documented cases of mass hysteria, you will find these types of environments to be typical; almost all cases of mass hysteria unfold in challenging, stressful environments, from impoverished villages in Africa to emergency rooms in large U.S. hospitals.

Why do people "catch" illusionary illnesses and follow others blindly down the street in particular environments but not others? Why does a certain individual—a stranger, a politician—have great impact when we are scared but not when we are relaxed? To answer these questions, we first need to understand what happens to our bodies and minds under threat.

Pressure, Pushing Down on Me

When we are under threat, a preprogrammed physiological reaction is triggered: stress. Evolution has equipped us with this response to help us survive. Imagine you are an antelope in the wild and you notice a lion running your way. Within seconds, stress hormones such as cortisol are secreted, triggering a chain reaction—your heart pumps overtime and your breath shortens. There are no spare resources to go around, so nonurgent functions must shut down; your immune system temporarily quiets, as do your digestive and reproductive systems. This is no time to deal with a healing wound or digest whatever you were chewing an hour ago; you must focus all your resources on one goal: surviving in the moment.

Humans are rarely put in the same kind of immediate danger as the antelope, yet we frequently experience stress. Whether it is in response to an unpaid mortgage, a deadline at work, or a strong competitor on a playing field, our bodies will release cortisol. Even a relatively benign situation, like being stuck in traffic during rush hour or in a slow queue at Starbucks, can trigger a full-blown stress reaction. The physical response will be similar to that observed in the antelope: the pulse and breathing rates will increase, and the function of systems that are not immediately required will decrease. If the stress is chronic, it will have a damaging effect on our bodies.[2] Our immune systems will weaken, and we'll become more susceptible to sickness; our digestion will slow, and as a result we'll become more likely to gain fat, especially around the midsection; our reproductive system will shut down, and as a long-term result, women may have difficulty conceiving.

Just as stress significantly alters the function of your heart, digestive system, immune system, and reproductive system, it also alters your brain. Every time you feel stress creeping up on you, the working of your brain dramatically changes. Within seconds, stress can alter the way you think, the way you make decisions, and the way you behave. And it changes the way you are influenced by those around you.

My students Neil Garrett, Ana Maria González-Garzón, and I devised an experiment to examine how exactly stress changes the way people are influenced by information. Our plan was simple: we would expose people to threat, record their physiological reactions, and observe how their thinking changed. Our first conundrum, however, was how best to induce a sense of threat in our volunteers. A hungry lion was out of the question, and so we decided to create the sort of stressful situation our volunteers might likely encounter in their own lives.

Imagine that you are a participant in our study. You arrive at our lab to take part in an experiment in exchange for a small fee. After you sign a consent form, Neil, the experimenter, asks you for a saliva sample. The request seems odd. "Why are they making me spit into a plastic tube?" you may ask. Well, from your saliva, Neil will measure the level of the stress hormone cortisol in your system before we even start the experiment. This is called a "baseline measure." Neil also asks you to fill out a short questionnaire to assess your current level of anxiety and records your baseline skin conductance level (SCL), which gives him another physiological way to determine your level of stress. At that point, you are likely still relaxed.

Neil then describes the experimental procedure to you. "First," he says, "you will complete a simple task on the computer, which will take about half an hour." "No problem," you say. "When you are done," he continues, "you will be given a piece of paper with a topic written on it. You will have five minutes to present the topic in front of a group of about thirty people. You will have no time to prepare, and your presentation will be recorded, so that others will be able to view it online."

To make sure you are indeed stressed out by all this, Neil again asks you to spit into a little tube so he can analyze your saliva; he also records your SCL and asks you to fill out a questionnaire measuring your anxiety level. If you are like most participants in our study, these measures will have risen from your baseline, indicating that we have successfully stressed you out.

We also had another group of participants in our study—the "control" group. Participants in this group were told that at the end of the study they would be asked to write a short essay on a surprise topic, but they were reassured that this was nothing to worry about, as their essay would neither be rated nor read by anyone. As expected, participants in this group did not exhibit signs of stress.

Now that half the students were anxious and the other half were calm, we were ready to conduct our test. We presented our volunteers with descriptions of dreadful events that could happen to them in the future, such as robbery, a car accident, or a broken rib. We then asked them how likely they thought these events were to happen to them. (For example: How likely are you to be robbed?) We then presented them with information regarding the likelihoods of these events in their population. (For example, we informed them that the likelihood of being robbed in London is about 30 percent.) Finally, we asked them again how likely they thought they were to experience those events. (How likely are you to be robbed?) With that data, we could then calculate how the information affected peoples' beliefs. We found that under threat, people were much more inclined to take in negative information—such as learning that the likelihood of being robbed is higher than they'd thought—than when they were relaxed.[3] The more stressed they were, the greater their tendency to alter their views in response to unexpected bad news. (Stress did not affect the ability of good news to change their beliefs.)

Under threat, we automatically absorb cues about danger. This is what happened to me when I observed a man running in Manhattan three days after 9/11 and to the anxious students in Arrabah. The same thing happened to the volunteers in our study when they received unsettling information just before having to give a public talk.

It wasn't just volunteers in the lab who reacted this way to our experiment. We ventured out of our lab in London and into fire stations in the state of Colorado. A firefighter's workday varies quite a bit. Some days are pretty relaxed; firefighters will spend most of such days in the station. Other days can be hectic, with numerous life-threatening incidents to attend to. For us, the ups and downs of calm and stress presented the perfect setting for an experiment. We figured that on days without many emergency calls, the firefighters would be calm and, as a result, attuned to "good news." Yet on days when they experienced constant threats, they would be anxious and more influenced by "bad news."

This is exactly what happened; the more stressed the firefighters felt while on duty, the more influenced they were by the unexpected bad news we gave them. The information we gave them (such as the likelihood of credit card fraud or robbery) had absolutely nothing to do with their work as firefighters, yet when they were under stress, any type of alarming news had a large impact.

Arguably, this mechanism has its advantages. If you are an antelope and your habitat is filled with hungry lions, you want to be alert to any indication that a predator may be near. The same is true if you are living in a violent neighborhood: heightened intake of *any* negative cues may help keep you alive. The problem is that this instinct can also cause us to overreact. For instance, people may buy hefty earthquake insurance after a quake in California, even if they are living in Iowa. Consider terrorist attacks, such as the one in Paris on November 13, 2015, as another example. The news of the attacks on civilians in the City of Light quickly spread globally. People everywhere feared for their own safety, and a worldwide panic ensued.[4] This, in turn, made people hypervigilant to any negative media reports, which, in turn, caused civilians to overestimate the danger to their own life. People then chose to "play it safe" for a while—to stay home rather than go out, to avoid visits to large cities.

In a similar manner, financial markets overreact to downturns—when the market shows an initial sign of a possible decline, people panic. Any information indicating even the slightest possibility of a downturn is given greater weight than it would have been previously. People then pull out of the market and the situation worsens, increasing investors' stress and inciting further panic, which increases attention to negative information, and so on. When we are stressed, we become fixated on detecting dangers; we focus on what can go wrong. This then creates excessively pessimistic views, which, in turn, can cause us to become overly conservative.

Playing It Safe

One particular environment where people's reactions to stress can be examined under the microscope is the playing field. Competitive sports give us a wonderful chance to observe how individuals behave under threat. When players are intimidated by their opponents, how do they respond?

Cue in our next leap.

The year: 2007. The place: Berkeley, California. The body: Jeff Tedford, the coach of the University of California Golden Bears. The Bears are on a winning streak. They have won five consecutive games in the first month of the college football season. By the time they come face-to-face with Oregon State in a homecoming game in Berkeley on October 13, they have climbed from number 15 at the beginning of the season to number 2 nationwide. This is their highest rank since 1951, and sixty-four thousand fans are in the stadium to support them. The teammates are elated. If they win the game today, they will conquer the top position, one they have not occupied in half a century.

Their luck, however, is about to run out. Two weeks earlier, at a game against the Oregon Ducks, the Golden Bears' quarterback, Nate Longshore, injured his ankle. Now, minutes before kickoff at the Berkeley stadium, their coach, Jeff Tedford, decides that Longshore is not fit to play. Kevin Riley, the inexperienced backup quarterback, will replace him. And with that move begins the Bears' slow and steady decline.

The game is tight. It comes down to the very last play; at fourteen seconds on the clock and third down, Kevin Riley finds himself facing a tough choice. He has the ball; either he can take the game into overtime by spiking it to set up a field goal or he can scramble toward the end zone. He has to make a split-second decision. "I knew there were fourteen seconds left on the clock. . . . I saw some green field, and I thought I could get around that guy. I was just using playing-ball instincts. I was in the middle of the play."[5]

He didn't make it to the end zone, and the Bears lost the critical game. Coach Tedford was seen throwing his clipboard down on the ground.

From that point on, the Bears' season made a sharp U-turn.

"Something changed that night . . . it is almost as if something snapped," observed one commentator.[6] Pressure quickly built on the shoulders of coach Tedford and the rest of the players. The Bears went on to lose five of their next six games, and with each loss, the stress grew. Down the ladder they went, from number 2 to number 9, then to number 20, and finally they dropped off the ladder altogether, ending the season unranked. Tedford "would never fully put a huge level of responsibility on a young, inexperienced player again"; he "felt he had to be overly conservative after that," speculated a fan.[7]

Coach Tedford went on to adopt a conservative, highly predictable approach, and "the Bears never again won a game where they were a significant underdog."[8] As another Bears supporter explained, "Tedford rarely loses games by more than two touchdowns. However, it also makes it tougher for us [the Bears] to beat USC, because we might be holding ourselves back from making too many mistakes to try and take the game at the end. . . . We have prided ourselves on close losses to USC."[9]

Once the Bears began losing, Tedford may have felt intimidated, and he started to play it safe. He was no anomaly. Examining over one thousand football games from 2002 to 2006, Brian Burke, the creator of Advanced NFL Stats, a website about football and game theory, found that underdog teams, like Tedford's, were less likely to vary their play. When they begin failing, they start minimizing risk. Burke hypothesizes that coaches "try to stay in the game for as long as possible. Underdog coaches minimize risk all game long hoping for a miracle along the way. They seem to be reducing the chances of being blown out."[10] Chris Brown, the author of *The Art of Smart Football*, agrees: "Almost every week of the season I see teams go to Southern Cal, LSU, or Ohio State [strong college football teams] and pretty much give up all hope of winning in the name of keeping it close and winning it in the fourth quarter."[11]

Both Brown and Burke are of the opinion that playing it safe is often the wrong approach for underdogs. Sure, a conservative strategy means underdog teams are less likely to fail grandiosely, but they are also less likely to win. The game will be predictable, with predictable strategies and predictable scores. So if you are the underdog and you're playing it safe, you will most likely lose. However, in risky games, outcomes are highly variable; the range of possible scenarios widens and encompasses more possibilities— including the chance of the risk paying off.

In the words of Brown, underdog teams "have little chance of winning on the merits, so what they need to do is . . . increase the chance for a shocker: take risks, and hope their coin flips go in their favor. Maybe they won't. Maybe they get blown out. But not taking those chances is a sure way to set their low chance of winning in stone."

Yet time and time again, teams like the California Golden Bears take the exact opposite approach. When they are high on their game, they take a chance and execute risky plays; when they are the underdog, they play it safe, shying away from the unpredictable as if it's fire.

Brown and Burke tried to find reasons for why underdogs fail to take risks when they should. Maybe a safe "near win" is better for a team's morale than taking a risk? Maybe the coach is trying to save his reputation by avoiding a blowout?

Maybe. I suspect there is another reason, though. To take a risk, you need to envision the possibility of it paying off; you need to be able to believe that winning is an option. When deciding on your next move, you consider the information in front of you and what that data tells you about the likelihood of different scenarios working out. However, as we saw earlier, once people feel threatened, they become more focused on the negative, and more likely to consider how things can go wrong. As a result, they decide that to act in a conservative manner even when taking a risk is, in fact, the better approach. Coach Tedford was simply being human; he was reacting to the stress of failure.

In situations that are life-threatening, avoiding risk can actually be the optimal approach. However, we also fall back on this instinct in situations where there are better decisions to be made. The good news is that we can overcome our instinct to play it safe when we are under stress. How? Cue in our next leap—into the body of Michael Chang.

How an Underdog Overcame Intimidation

Monday, June 5, 1989. On the tennis courts of the Stade Roland Garros in Paris, a seventeen-year-old Asian-American was getting ready to serve. His name was Michael Chang, and he was seeded fifteenth in the French Open. On the other side of the court was the Czech player Ivan Lendl. Ivan was twelve years Michael's senior, which made him far more experienced. At six foot two, he was also physically larger than the slight, five-foot-nine Chang. Most importantly, Lendl was ranked number 1 in the world; he came to the French Open after winning the Australian Open and numerous other tournaments that year.

"Chang wasn't in his league," said Bud Collins, who was covering the game for the *Boston Globe* and NBC.[12] He was the underdog—it was as simple as that.

This was not the first time Chang and Lendl had found themselves on opposite sides of the court. A year earlier, they had met in

Des Moines, Iowa, where Lendl had beat Chang without batting an eye.

"Do you want to know why I beat you today?" asked Lendl back in Iowa. "Truthfully, you've got nothing that can hurt me. You've got no serve; your second serve is not very strong. So, pretty much whenever I play you, I can do whatever I want, however I want, and I am going to beat you pretty comfortable like I did today."

Chang seemed to take Lendl's words to heart and spent the next year working on his serve, hitting the ball harder, moving it better.[13] His labor began to pay off. While Lendl easily took the first two sets on the French court, Chang managed to win the next two. Yet the effort took its toll on the youngster. Playing at full force for over three hours left him weak and dehydrated. He tried to compensate by constantly fueling his svelte body with water and bananas and choosing energy-conserving moves.

"Toward the end of the fourth set, I started to cramp anytime I had to run really hard. So I resorted to hitting a lot of moon balls, and trying to keep points as short as possible," said Chang.[14]

But his body was failing him. A small step forward felt as challenging as climbing the Himalayas, moving his arm to hit the ball as difficult as lifting a trolley track. He decided to call it a day: "I couldn't serve, I couldn't dig out any balls that were hit in the corners and I walked to the service line, to basically tell the umpire I can't play anymore, I'm done."[15] Chang's intuitive reaction was to go home, to retreat to his safe zone. But then he reconsidered.

Seconds before reaching the umpire, he had a change of heart: "It dawned on me that if I was to quit then and there, every other difficult time I have there on the court it was just going to make it that much easier to quit. And from there, it wasn't so much a matter of winning and losing, my objective that day was to finish the race which was that match, which was that fifth set. Win or lose I had to finish the match."[16] He turned back to complete the fifth and final set, which would decide the game.

You can probably guess what happened next. The inspirational story of the small fry taking on the giant is not, however, the reason I am recounting this tale. Regardless of whether Chang won or lost, his next couple of decisions made him an anomaly.

Falling behind 15–30 and still struggling physically, Chang decided to take a series of unconventional risks. His next actions had a high probability of failure and could come at dire cost—if he failed, he would seem foolish and inexperienced to the world. But if he were to succeed, the reward would be tremendous: the second-generation, Hoboken-born teen would be triumphant.

Chang chose an unusual tactic: "Spur of the moment, I was just like, I'm going to throw an underhand serve in here, 'cause I'm not doing anything off my first serve anyways. Let's see if maybe I can scrape a point."[17] Instead of attempting a fast, strong serve, he hit the ball like a child.

It worked. The underhand serve took Lendl by surprise, leaving the score at 30 all. Encouraged, Chang decided to try one more trick. "I had two match points," he figured, "so I might as well take a crack."[18] Chang slowly started walking forward toward the service line, trying to distract Lendl with this unusual move. The crowd responded with laughs and hoots. Lendl, confused, ended up serving a double fault. The game was Chang's, and he went on to win the French Open. He was the first American male to win a Grand Slam singles tournament in five years.

As we have seen earlier, when people are intimidated, they tend to avoid risky moves and adopt a conservative approach; they do not take chances like Chang. What, then, helped Chang overcome the typical actions of the underdog?

When asked what motivated him to take risks, Chang attributed his regained psychological strength to the events at Tiananmen Square the evening before his match. On June 4, 1989, thousands of unarmed civilian protestors lost their lives when trying to block the Chinese military's advance into the square. Chang watched the

Figure 6.1. State. *Watch out for the influence of others on your emotional state. Being stressed or intimidated changes the way we process information and make decisions. One consequence is that we start to "play it safe," even when taking a risk is the best approach. For example, when sport teams are the underdogs, they play over-conservatively, when, in fact, their best bet would be to take risks. Being mindful of this automatic influence of others on our decisions can enable us to overcome it when needed by reframing the situation in a different light. For example, when Chang played against the stronger, more experienced Lendl, he decided to view the match as an opportunity to make history.*

events on TV the night before he faced Lendl on the court. The tragedy could have demotivated him and increased his anxiety. Yet the reverse happened. Rather than hinder his spirits, the events in Tiananmen Square caused Chang to think about the tennis match not as a lost cause but, in his words, as "an opportunity to bring a smile upon Chinese people's faces around the world when there wasn't a whole lot to smile about."[19] Chang was actively reframing the situation in his mind, focusing on opportunity even under threat. He kept that thought in mind on the court, and the rest is history.

Humans, probably unlike any other animal, have the capacity to consciously direct their inner attention to different aspects of the situation and overcome their automatic reactions. In one study, for example, volunteers were shown a horror movie that caused them to be scared. Sure enough, when asked to make monetary decisions shortly after, they were more likely to avoid financial risk, even if the stakes were in their favor.[20] But here is the twist: when volunteers were instructed to reappraise the movie, to think about it differently in order to undo the fear—perhaps to keep in mind that it was only a movie—they became more open to taking a risk.[21] In other words, we can consciously alter our emotional state to overcome instinctive patterns. How does this happen in the brain? To understand this, we will take one final leap—this time into the mind of Laurie, an undergraduate at the California Institute of Technology.

Taming the Amygdala

The California Institute of Technology in Pasadena, California, attracts some of the brightest minds in the world; thirty-four of its alumni have received the Nobel Prize, and many have gone on to found leading companies. The competitive environment, however, can also create considerable stress on the young students. How does such pressure affect the students' academic performance? And what makes one student succumb to the stress but another overcome it?

To answer this question, a team of scientists invited Caltech students into their lab in groups of five.[22] Albert, Robert, Marie, Laurie, and William arrived at the lab and took an IQ test. Their exams were scored and documented. All five did extremely well, with an average score of 126. (For comparison, the average IQ in the general population is 100.)

A few weeks later, the students came back to take the test again. This time, however, there was a twist: while they took the exam, the students were shown their current rank in the group. At first, everyone's scores plummeted. The fear of social humiliation and the stress of competition interfered with their ability to think clearly. However, as the test progressed, Albert and Laurie managed to shake off the anxiety and concentrate on the task at hand. In fact, they became motivated to do better than the others, and their final scores actually rose. The other students, however, were not able to recover and ended up with scores that were lower than before.

The students' brains were scanned while they were taking the test, and to find out what made Albert and Laurie react differently from the rest of the group, the scientists studied those scans. The readouts showed that activity in two brain structures was critical: the amygdala and the frontal lobes. As discussed in earlier chapters, the amygdala is that deep-brain structure important for processing emotions, such as fear, as well as social signals. The frontal lobes are crucial for, among other functions, planning, high cognitive activities, and controlling our emotions.[23] Everyone had high amygdala activity at first. But Albert's and Laurie's amygdala activity decreased rapidly, while the activity in their frontal lobes increased. Presumably, they were able to cognitively tame the fear and focus on the task at hand. In contrast, amygdala activity in the rest of the students remained high. It seems that Albert and Laurie, similar to Chang, were able to overcome social intimidation and refocus. The others remained intimidated, and it hurt their performance.

On Sunshine and Gambling

I suspect that many of the students were unaware that fear was affecting their test scores. Most of us do not realize how our emotional reactions alter our minds; it happens outside our awareness. Yet the hidden influence of our emotional state is far-reaching—it is not only a negative emotional state, such as stress, that changes people's thinking and decisions; positive states can affect our choices as well.

One striking demonstration comes from a study looking at the sales of lottery tickets. The likelihood of winning the lottery is ridiculously low. So what causes a person to go out and purchase a ticket? Well, one contributing factor seems to be mood. Examining lottery sales in New York City, Ross Otto and his colleagues from New York University stumbled on a peculiar pattern.[24] When unexpected good events happened, more people bought lottery tickets. A local sports team unexpectedly won a game? Purchases escalated. An atypical sunny day in the midst of winter? Sales went up.* This study is correlational—it shows a relationship between variables, but we do not know whether one factor is driving

---

* The authors claim that this could not be attributed simply to people being more likely to be out and about, as a typical sunny day in June did not have the same effect. The assumption is that an atypical sunny day makes us happier than a typical one.

another. However, one theory is that an unexpected positive event, such as a bright, sunny day, makes people feel good. When you are joyful and relaxed, your mind is more likely to focus on how things may go your way. You may then overestimate your luck and be more inclined to take a risk.

* * *

Mass hysteria in New York City and Arrabah, an NFL coach playing it safe under threat, and firefighters attuned to negative information—all of these examples highlight the fact that influence is about more than the message or the messenger. A critical component is the mental state of the receiver. People's emotional states can completely alter their thinking, decisions, and interactions. Your friend Snooky may be convinced by an argument you are making if she happens to be anxious that day, but unaffected if she happens to be relaxed. Under different emotional states, people are primed to attend to particular cues. This principle is important to keep in mind. It explains, for example, why fear campaigns can be useless in a certain time and place, yet effective in another. If you are attempting to give advice—to a player on a winning streak, a patient who has just received a dire diagnosis, or a client in the midst of a divorce—you need to pull a "Sam Beckett": leap from your reality into that of the other to assess their emotional state. A person's emotional mind-set will affect how they react to what you have to say. There needs to be a match between the opinions we are offering and the state of the individual in front of us. The same person will ignore your guidance one day but welcome it with open arms another, simply because their favorite football team lost last night or because the sun is shining on a winter day.

7

⸻◈⸻

Why Do Babies Love iPhones?
(Others, Part I)

The Strength of Social Learning and the
Pursuit of Uniqueness

On a bright April day, I found myself at the labor ward of a London hospital alternating between high-pitched violent screams and a civilized search for baby names. Scarlett? Dotty? Isabella? Between one excruciatingly painful contraction and the next, my husband and I had three minutes of relative clarity in which to attend to the important task of naming our unborn daughter. Zoe was cute, but would it fit our daughter if she grew up to become a CEO? Theodora was classy but too serious. We were determined not to let our tiny bundle of blood and joy enter the world nameless. It wasn't that we were relentless procrastinators, leaving this crucial task to the last minute. No, for the past few months we had spent hours each night debating the options. We wanted a name that was meaningful, sophisticated, and easy to spell and pronounce, did not remind us of anyone that was less than perfect, was unique but not weird, and would fit both a rock star and a president (just in case).

Anxious and naïve, as first-time parents often are, we wanted to give our daughter a great start. In our minds, there was a lot at stake. The name would be the first part of her identity, portraying our expectations of what that little person would become. As behavioral scientists, we knew perfectly well how expectations can become self-fulfilling.* Expectations wrapped up in a name, we thought, could affect how our daughter would view herself and how others would perceive her. Research shows that girls with feminine names, such as Elizabeth, are more likely to study humanities, while girls with masculine-sounding names, such as Alexis, are more inclined to choose math; boys with "girly" names, such as Morgan, are more likely to have behavioral problems; and children with names traditionally given by underprivileged parents are treated differently than their siblings with posh-sounding names like Sebastian. If that were not enough, a study of three thousand parents published in 2010 revealed that one parent in five ended up regretting the name they gave their child.[1] To what extent do names really affect people's life? We were not sure, but we decided not to take any chances.

These considerations did not occur to us at first. We thought that naming our daughter would be an easy feat. Shortly after discovering that we were having a girl, we agreed we liked the sound of Sophia. It had an Old World ring to it and means "goddess of wisdom." Perfect. We were blissfully happy with fetus Sophia. That is, until my husband decided to look at the list of the one

---

* The science on the relationship between names and life outcomes is mixed. In their wonderful book *Freakonomics*, Steven D. Levitt and Stephen J. Dubner present data suggesting that a name reflects the parents' expectations and has no causal effect (direct or indirect) on the baby's life. Nevertheless, we decided to play it safe and pick what Levitt and Dubner call a "winner" name.

hundred most popular baby names. To our utter devastation, at the very top of the list was Sophia. Apparently the rest of the world felt exactly as we did about our wonderfully sophisticated name.

We were astonished. Up until that point, we'd been convinced that we had unique tastes, a different way of thinking, and an unusual perception of the world around us. Well, a quick scroll down the list put an end to all that. Not only were we about to give our daughter the most common name, according to the U.S. Social Security Administration statistics of 2013, but every other name on our runners-up list was in the U.S. *and* the U.K. top ten. Olivia? Tick. Emma? Tick. Mia? Tick. Who knew we were just like everyone else? We were blissfully unaware that billions of others around the globe shared our tastes, and that our strong sense of individuality might have been an illusion.

Why do seemingly diverse humans have similar preferences? Sophia cannot be objectively better than the thousands of other names out there. Neither is it the case that we were all making a conscious decision to follow a trend. So why were so many people making the same decision at the same time?

Social Learning from Day One

After twenty hours of screaming, sweating, and swearing in the labor ward, I was more interested in painkillers than naming my unborn daughter. So I left her fate in the trusted hands of my husband. From our short list of finalists he choose Livia (Livia was the feisty wife of the Roman emperor Augustus). And so gutsy little Livia was born and quickly progressed from crying to smiling to sitting to crawling. A few months before she turned one, my friend Nick came to visit. He enthusiastically told me of the *doljanchi* ceremony he had attended the previous week. *Doljanchi* is a Korean tradition for celebrating a child's first birthday. The best part of the *doljanchi*, Nick said, is the fortune-telling ritual. The unsuspecting baby is placed in front of an assortment of objects and is encouraged to pick one. The selection is believed to forecast the child's future: if the baby picks up a banana, she will never go hungry; a book means she is destined for academia; a silver coin foretells wealth; a paintbrush, creativity.

I was intrigued. That very same evening, I placed Livia in front of a collection of items: a stethoscope (would she become a doctor?), a stuffed dog (a vet?), a plant (a Greenpeace activist?), a piece of pastry (a chef?), and a colorful model of the brain (a neuroscientist?). Livia inspected the options closely, took her time, and then went straight for the iPhone I had happened to leave at the corner of the table.

I shouldn't have been surprised. The little girl was obsessed with this piece of machinery. She would skillfully roll herself from one side of the room to the other to grab hold of it. Such a maneuver would make perfect sense if she would then check her e-mail or update her Facebook status. That, however, was not her intention. When she finally grabbed hold of the phone, she would quickly insert it into her mouth and attempt to chew. Eating the iPhone proved unsuccessful, yet she was not discouraged. Time and time again she would reach for the phone, even if there were edible items in sight. It was not the noise or the lights that intrigued her; she had other bright musical toys that she did not desire as much. The iPhone was the item she wanted because from the day she was born, she had observed her parents constantly interacting with it with great interest. Although she was only a few months old, and could not even say a word, she was able to infer that these metal rectangles must be extremely valuable.

Little Livia's fondness for iPhones tells us something important about how our brains work. It suggests that we are born with an automatic predisposition to learn from those around us. The tendency is instinctive, a reflex—an impulse for social learning.

The human brain is engineered to acquire knowledge within a social context. We learn almost everything—from what item is most valuable to how to peel an orange—from observing other people's behavior. We imitate, assimilate, and adopt; and we often do this without awareness. The advantage of this setup is that we need not learn only from our own limited experiences with the environment but can also pick up information or techniques from the experience of many others. This means that we can learn quickly, rather than only through the slow process of trial and error.

We learn by observing another person live—as my daughter did from watching her parents interact with their phones—or via a screen, as through social media, films, and television. For example, the recent popularity of the name Mason in the United States can be traced back to Mason Disick, the son of reality TV personalities Kourtney Kardashian and Scott Disick. While the name's popularity was already growing, a year after Disick's birth it jumped from number 34 on the top 100 list to number 2 and has not dipped below number 4 in five years. You do not even need to be familiar with the series to be affected; as James Fowler and Nicholas Christakis beautifully explain in their book *Connected*, influence travels from person to person. Of course, we cannot prove cause and effect here—Mason Disick may have had nothing to do with the popularity growth of his name but, rather, may reflect it. (In other words, his parents may themselves have been influenced by a growing trend.) However, the fact that many popular names experience a boost immediately following the appearance in the media of a character, real or fictitious, bearing that name suggests that causation is likely. (In case you were wondering, name experts are still debating the origins of Sophia's popularity.)

And yet almost all of us say we are less likely to be influenced by others than the next person. This, of course, is statistically impossible. We cannot all be less susceptible than the average Joe. The reason we view ourselves as little versions of Mahatma Gandhi is that influence often works under the radar. In fact, what most of us say we desire is to be different. The notion that we are the product of others' preferences is uncomfortable. Our conscious drive for individuality, together with our unconscious aptitude for social learning, leads us to converge on the same "distinct" choices.

Think Different?

In July 1997 Craig Tanimoto, an art director at TBWA\Chiat\Day advertising agency, had the task of coming up with an ad campaign for personal computers. His client, a hardware company, had a good product, but they were struggling with sales. Although artsy types were purchasing their computers, the crowds were buying IBM ThinkPads. The company needed to reach the masses if they were to survive.[2] How could Craig sway people to abandon IBM and buy into his client's products?

Three other teams at Craig's agency were also trying to come up with innovative solutions. After a week of brainstorming, they all came together to present their proposals. Rob Siltanen, the creative director of TBWA\Chiat\Day at the time, recalled a conference room covered from floor to ceiling with sketches, photos, and signs.[3] Most of the ideas were mundane and uninspiring. But Craig's proposal stood out. Craig had put together black-and-white images of extraordinary people: one of Thomas Edison, a second of Albert Einstein, a third of Mahatma Gandhi. At the top of each photo he'd inserted the words "Think different" and the rainbow-colored Apple logo. Simple, yet brilliant.

The "Think different" campaign was to become a huge success. It won every award and made Apple's sales skyrocket. Everyone wanted to think just like Edison or Einstein, and if Macintosh was the answer, so be it. Today, half of all U.S. homes own an Apple product, and, ironically, it was the "Think different" campaign that kick-started the frenzy. What Craig had tapped into was a basic human desire—to be unique, yet trendy. The paradox, of course, is that while we like to see ourselves as different, we are also quick to adopt the views and preferences of those around us; the sort of music we listen to, the type of people we befriend, the technology we use, and the names we give our children are not decisions we make independently.

This tendency is often portrayed as a weakness; our lack of independence may mean that we trade our own goals for those of others, which may not be right for us. It is a legitimate concern, one that I will return to later. But turn the tables around and you will see that social learning can be an incredible opportunity, a tool for positively affecting the people around you simply by modeling a desired behavior. Display the right choices and you will increase the likelihood that others will choose the same. However, make poor ones and others may, too.

If Anyone Orders Merlot—I'm Leaving!

One of the clearest demonstrations of the power of social learning is still the original experiment conducted by Stanford psychologist Albert Bandura in the early 1960s. Bandura invited seventy-two preschoolers from the Stanford nursery school to participate in his study.[4] One of the participants was little James. When James arrived at the lab, he was seated at the corner of a playroom with stickers and stamps to occupy him. In the other corner was Harold, a researcher working on Bandura's team. Harold quietly played with some toys for a few minutes. Then, suddenly, out of nowhere he began to beat an inflated doll that had been placed next to him. "Pow wow!" cried Harold.

James observed the commotion for a while and was then taken to another room filled with toys. He joyfully interacted with the trucks and blocks he found there, only to be told a short while later that he must go back to the first room. Frustrated, James started hitting the inflated doll upon his return. "Pow wow!" cried James.

Another little kid participating in the study was Eddie. Eddie had a similar experience to James's, with one exception; when Eddie was in the room with Harold, Harold did not act aggressively. As a result, Eddie did not act violently, either. Yes, Eddie was also frustrated by having to leave the truck-filled room behind, but he did not express this frustration with aggression. James and Eddie represent participants in the two experimental groups in Bandura's study. Those who observed violent behaviors were much more likely to later display the same. Those who did not witness Harold hitting the doll did not do so themselves.

We are all Harolds. We may not be aware of it, but the way we behave is perceived by others and then imitated. This is true in almost every situation, but it is especially true in situations where others are paying close attention—mentees, kids, colleagues, and friends. We provide signals to others on what is normative, what is desirable. If children, for example, constantly observe adults on their phones eating salty chips, it will be extremely difficult to convince them to instead read a book while eating a pear. However, select fruit over chips, and others in your vicinity may do the same.

Take, for instance, an experiment a student of mine, Caroline

Charpentier, and I conducted.[5] We asked one hundred volunteers to come to our lab at the center of London after fasting all day: no greasy English breakfast, no much-needed cup of coffee, no mid-day snack. The students arrived famished. At that point, we asked them to rate eighty different food items, from baked beans to apples and wasabi peas. They then made multiple selections from the items, having been told that we would give them their picks at the end of the study. Just before they were about to make their choices, we presented them with what other students, who had participated in the study earlier, had selected. At the end of the study, we asked if they thought they had been influenced by the food choices of the other participants.

This is what one student said: "I was interested and occasionally surprised to see what others chose but my preferences stayed the same!" Another argued, "It was their choice and did not influence me in making my own choices."

Like most of our participants, these two were completely wrong. Looking at the first participant's behavior, we found that 20 percent of the time she picked a food item that she'd initially said she did not like at all (such as cherry tomatoes), after learning that others had chosen it (the second student did the same thing 10 percent of the time). That means that for one in five choices she made, she decided to eat something she'd previously said she did not want, because of social learning.* When people perceive others' choices, the brain automatically encodes added utility to those selected options in regions that are important for signaling value. Our brains operate according to the rule that what is desired by others is likely valuable. Then later, when it is time to make a

---

* We also had a control condition that ensured that these odd choices were indeed due to social learning and not to random "noise" in the subjects' ratings or lack of attention.

choice, we retrieve these value signals unconsciously and use them to make a decision.

A wonderful example of this comes from a fictional character who had a tremendous impact on the very real sales of wine.[6] In 2004 the world met Miles, a wine connoisseur on a tour of wineries in Santa Barbara County, California. Miles, a heartbroken divorcé played by Paul Giamatti in the movie *Sideways*, was on a last hurrah with his friend Jack, who was about to be married. The film did wonders for the sales of Santa Barbara wines. Except for one variety: merlot.

"If anyone orders merlot, I'm leaving, I am NOT drinking any f——ing merlot!" With that single line in the movie, Miles inflicted damage on the sales of merlot for over a decade. This effect has yet to be reversed. Miles opted for pinot noir instead, for which sales have since skyrocketed. Simply observing a person making a choice— naming their kid Mason or drinking pinot noir—results in those options seeming more valuable and more likely to be chosen by others. This is true even if the person making the choice is merely the product of another's imagination.

The Wrong Inference

The concern with social learning is that at times we will be influencing others to make decisions that are not best for them. Take Livia, for example. Livia would have been better off choosing the pastry, which she could chew on, or the stuffed dog, which she could play with. But she did not want the things that fit her needs; she wanted the one item that fit mine—my phone. I worried that she would still be confusing the two in twenty years, when it came time to pick a job or a life partner.

The situation might have been different if Livia and I were

living thousands of years ago in the forest with our hunter-gatherer ancestors. Back then, food was scarce and highly valuable to all, and so the needs of one person were more aligned with those of another: nourishment, warmth, shelter. Going after what was deemed valuable by another would often be the optimal strategy. Fast-forward to today and the situation is somewhat different. In our plentiful world of cupcakes and T-bone steaks, the basic needs of most humans in the Western world are met. The items now deemed valuable are not necessarily crucial for survival. In our specialized, customized world, the items I cherish are not necessarily of much use to you.

Following someone else's choice can be harmless; however, it can also be life-threatening. Here is one such striking example: every year, 10 percent of kidney donations in the United States go unused. It turns out that when a donation is declined by one patient, whether because of the patient's specific medical condition or their religious beliefs, the next patient on the list is informed that the organ was previously declined but is not told the reason. That patient then assumes that the organ is faulty and passes up a potentially lifesaving operation—as will the next patient, and the next. Replace "kidneys" with "real estate," "romantic partners," "financial stocks," or "professional projects," and it becomes apparent how often people pass on opportunities that may benefit them due to past choices of other people.[7]

This is true both offline and online. Consider popular websites—many quantify and display the opinion of other people in a digestible manner. It's a candy store for the social-learning brain, full of lollipops and marshmallows in the form of ratings and comments. For example, at the time of writing, scrolling down the nation's one hundred most viewed websites, you'll find Facebook at number 3, Amazon at number 5, Twitter at number 10,

Figure 7.1. Others. *Be mindful of (over) social learning.* Our instinct is to imitate the choices of others, because we assume that others have information we do not. However, other people's decisions can stem from considerations that are irrelevant to us. We need to be careful when following others' choices, mindful that they may not be right for us. For example, one out of ten kidney donations go unused in the United States, because after they have been rejected by one patient, other patients are more likely to pass, even when the organ is a good fit for them.

Pinterest at number 15. Going further down the list, you'll come upon Yelp, TripAdvisor, and Reddit. You've probably visited one of these sites today. I have. All these websites help us decide where to vacation, which of our friends we like, which book we should read next, and which physician we should avoid. There are even dating websites in which women rate the man they went out with last night for the benefit of other women. Ratings are the new bible—a guide for living. The question is, how good a guide are they?

We assume that online ratings are a reflection of the opinions of many independent users and we give them great weight. But there is something we do not take into account. When you rate a restaurant on Yelp, a book on Amazon, or a hotel on TripAdvisor, you are not staring at a blank slate. At the time of the rating, you have already been presented with the existing ratings of that restaurant or book or hotel, and those ratings will affect your own. Sean Taylor, who received his PhD from NYU and now works for Facebook, has studied how existing ratings and comments influence subsequent ratings.[8] He found that if you manipulate the ratings so that the *first* review is glowing, the likelihood of other positive reviews increases by 32 percent and the final rating is enhanced by 25 percent! This means that the difference between a restaurant with an average rating and one with a phenomenal rating can sometimes be attributed to the first person who happened to log on and register their opinion. The ability of one person, one rating, to influence so many others that follow is quite remarkable.

These ratings do matter for people's life decisions. For example, a few weeks ago I was helping one of my students select courses for the fall semester. I suggested a social psychology course that might help with his research. My student looked up the professor who was teaching the course on www.ratemyprofessors.com. After learning that the professor's ratings were low, he decided to pass and take an anthropology course instead, since that class would be taught by a lecturer who'd received top scores. My student was making important educational decisions, with potentially long-lasting effects, based on numbers that might not reflect as much as they seem to. He was also ignoring the possibility that while the typical student might not have appreciated the course, the class might have fit his unique interests.

Inside the Brain

A couple of years ago, at the Weizmann Institute of Science in Israel, Micah Edelson, Yadin Dudai, and I decided to investigate what goes on inside the brain when we learn of the opinions and beliefs of others. What exactly changes, physically, in the brain?

Imagine you are a participant in our study. On a Monday morning you arrive at Yadin's lab, a modern building at the center of a sunny green campus about a twenty-minute drive from Tel Aviv. You take a seat in the waiting room, where you meet Rosie, Danielle, Sue, and Adam. They will be participating in the study with you. Micah, the experimenter, enters the room. He asks everyone to fill out a few forms and then screens a documentary. The movie lasts about forty-five minutes; it depicts the hardships of illegal immigrants in Tel Aviv. It is a little-known fact, but a large number of illegal immigrants arrive in Israel every year to work as caregivers, in construction, and in the restaurant industry. The police had established a special unit to track them down, and the movie details the emotional story of the friction between the police officers and the immigrants.

After the movie is over, you sit down in front of a computer and take a test involving two hundred questions about the movie. What color dress was the woman wearing when she got arrested? (You think it is red.) How many policemen were there at the time? (Probably two.) And so on. Adam, Rosie, and the other participants are also taking the test. Everyone does pretty well. A few days later, you are invited back to the lab. This time your brain will be scanned while you take the test again in an MRI scanner. For this test, however, before you decide on each answer, you are shown the responses of Adam, Rosie, Sue, and Danielle. Unbeknownst to you, in some instances you are being presented with fake answers—and they're purposely wrong.

Here we go. What color dress was the woman wearing when she got arrested? You think it is red, but Adam, Rosie, Danielle, and Sue all say white. What do you do? Astonishingly, 70 percent of the time, people go along with the wrong answers given by others. Although these participants thought they knew the truth, their confidence was shattered by the group.

That's not all. At the end of the test, we reveal to our participants that, in fact, some of the answers given by Sue, Danielle, Adam, and Rosie were fake. We then ask the participants to take the test one more time, and to please answer the questions according to their own memories.

This is where things become really interesting. The manipulation was so powerful that half of our volunteers' memories are changed forever—they now have inaccurate recollections of the movie and are stuck with the wrong answer.[9] When asked if they thought they were still being influenced by the fake answers we had shown them before, almost uniformly their response was "No!" What was going on?

The key to the puzzle was a brain region that you may remember from the previous chapters: the amygdala. Most species, from mice to macaques, have an amygdala; it is part of our evolutionarily "old" brain. The amygdala is well known for its role in processing emotions, such as fear.[10] But what most people don't know is that when the function of the amygdala was first reported, it was thought to be related not to emotion but to social processing. In the late 1930s two scientists, Heinrich Klüver and Paul Bucy, reported that monkeys with lesions to the medial temporal lobe (where the amygdala sits) would suddenly engage in inappropriate social behaviors.[11] We now know that it is not just monkeys that need an intact amygdala in order to have a normal social life. Humans do, too, because the ability to process emotion is closely intertwined with social skills. It turns out that if you have a large amygdala, you are likely to have more friends, multifaceted social networks, and are probably better at making accurate social judgments about people.[12]

What we found in our study was that when a volunteer learned of other people's answers to the test questions, their amygdala was activated. The amygdala then communicated with a nearby region that is essential for creating memories—the hippocampus—and that interaction resulted in changes to how the person remembered the film.[13]

We found that these socially induced changes to memory could subsequently be corrected by frontal lobe activity.[14] When participants in our experiment later discovered that we had provided them with the fake recollections of others, those with highly active frontal lobes were able to recover their original memory of the movie. But this correction did not always work. When your amygdala reacts very strongly to other people's opinions, it triggers a biological reaction that prevents your frontal lobes from subsequently correcting false beliefs.

When the volunteers in our experiment went along with the false recollections of others, about half the time they truly came to believe that those recollections were correct. They were not simply agreeing to save face or avoid conflict; their memory trace was physically altered. A great advantage of looking at brain activity when people are influenced by others is that we can detect when a change in belief, memory, or preference is likely to be a true modification and when a person just finds it easier to agree with the majority even though deep down they know the truth.

Who Will Jump First?

When your opinions and decisions are observed by others, they will make a difference. Accepting a job offer, rejecting a romantic partner, giving a hotel a top rating, passing on an organ donation—all of these can change others' perceptions and decisions. However, there is another critical factor that determines whether your choice will influence that of others: the visible consequences of those decisions.

Take the case of the Adélie penguins, described by the economist Christophe Chamley.[15] The Adélies are small penguins that live in Antarctica. With their black bodies and large white tummies, they resemble toddling tuxedos. They are often found strolling in large groups toward the edge of the water in search of food. Krill are a favorite. Yet danger awaits in the icy-cold water. There is the leopard seal, for one, which likes to have penguins for an entrée. The penguins' big white tummies are gurgling, but so is the seal's. What is an Adélie to do?

The penguins' solution is to play the waiting game. They wait and wait and wait by the edge of the water until one of them gives up and jumps (or is pushed) in. The moment that occurs, the rest of the penguins stretch their little necks as far as they possibly can. They watch with anticipation to see what happens next. If the pioneer survives, everyone else will follow suit. If it perishes, they'll turn away. One penguin's destiny alters the fate of all the others. Their strategy, you could say, is "learn and live."

We tall two-legged creatures do the same thing. We watch our risk-seeking pal jump and wait to see if they land safely before taking the plunge ourselves. This is true both literally—people will wait until someone else jumps off a diving board or over a gate before doing so themselves—and figuratively—we are more likely to start a company, write a book, divorce, or have a child if we see someone else do the same thing and end up on the right side of the fence. Observation is a good strategy even if we are simply choosing a glass of wine. Watching other people's reaction as they sip their preferred red is not a bad policy for deciding which bottle to order.

In short, people observe not only your choices but also the consequences you experience as a result of those choices. This is why rewarding people for good behavior and punishing them for bad behavior has widespread consequences—it affects not only the person being praised or critiqued but also everyone else who is watching. To prove this point, Albert Bandura, the psychologist we met earlier, followed up his inflated-doll experiment with a similar study in which Harold either received candy after hitting the doll or was told never to do it again. The children in the study were more likely to punch the inflated doll if they had observed Harold being rewarded and less likely if they saw him being told off.[16]

How does the human brain learn from the consequences of others' actions? Do we simply utilize the same neural system we use to learn from our own experiences? Or have we evolved a parallel mechanism to learn from another's success and failures? From experiments in monkeys, we know that the neurons that respond to our own mistakes and triumphs are not the same ones that responded to another's. These cells sit next to each other, but they are not one unit.[17] The distinction is helpful, as it allows us to differentiate our own mishaps from those of others, yet to learn from both.

There is another difference in how your brain reacts to your own experiences relative to others'. It is one that perhaps reveals an unpleasant side to human nature. Deep in your brain lies the striatum. It is an evolutionarily old part of the brain that is important, among other things, for learning about what can bring us joy and what may bring us harm. Dopaminergic neurons in the striatum tend to do this by enhancing their firing when outcomes are better than expected (this increases the likelihood that you will repeat the action that led to the good outcome) and reducing their firing when outcomes are worse than expected (inhibiting the likelihood that you will repeat the action that led to the bad outcome).[18]

For instance, imagine you are back in college and your professor asks you a tough question. You are unsure of the answer but manage to mumble some kind of reply. "Well done!" says the professor. "That is the most articulate answer I have heard all semester. You get extra credit!" The neurons in your striatum go crazy. They immediately increase their firing, indicating that the professor's positive feedback was pleasant and unexpected. On the other hand, if the professor says, "Really, that is pure nonsense—I am so disappointed. I will have to give you a failing grade!," your striatal neurons will reduce their firing, indicating that the professor's feedback was unpleasant and unexpected.

Here is the interesting thing though: studies show that if it was not you the professor singled out but your friend Maximus, the neurons in your striatum will show the opposite pattern of response.[19] They will enhance their firing if Maximus was told off and reduce their firing if Maximus was praised. Perhaps your brain perceives others as competitors and, therefore, codes their mistakes as rewarding to the self, and their successes as a loss.

The important point, though, is that you are able to learn from Maximus's experience and he from yours, and that is a great thing. In fact, your mind does more than just encode Maximus's experience; it often compares Maximus's behavior to how you imagine you would have reacted. When observing a coworker give a presentation or a friend cook dinner, we frequently engage in ongoing comparison. "Oh, I would not have presented that graph as a pink bar chart" or "That is way too much salt for a fettuccine Alfredo—I wonder what he is thinking." Many times your "what if" decisions are compatible with the other person's life decisions. But when their action does not fit the one you expected to take yourself, the incompatibility will cause neurons in your frontal lobe (specifically in a region called the dorsolateral prefrontal cortex) to fire.[20] The neurons are saying, "Hey, something here is unexpected, and we all need to take note." This signal draws extra attention to what is going on: someone made a different decision than you would have, and it is an opportunity to observe whether their decision was a good one.

Theory of Mind

As we have seen, our brains are set up to habitually learn from others. We imitate from the day we are born, we automatically reevaluate items based on others' choices, our memories change to align with others', and our neurons code for the mishaps and triumphs of everyone around us. There is one more trick our brains use for this purpose; it is known as theory of mind.[21]

I am writing these words on February 14, also known as Valentine's Day. You may adopt the cynical view that "the day was invented by chocolatiers to make an extra buck" or the more romantic notion that "this is an opportunity to remind the person who tolerates me every day how much I love them." The truth is, if you are in any sort of relationship, you probably know that it does not matter what you think of Valentine's Day. What matters is what your partner thinks. Yes, you can ask them directly, but they probably want you to figure it out on your own. So what really determines if your valentine is happy is what you think they think of the tradition. Your task is then to put yourself in the pants—or high-heeled shoes—of your partner to uncover their expectations. That, in essence, is "theory of mind"—our ability to think about what other people are thinking. We seem to be the only species on earth that can do this; we think constantly about what our client, patient, employee, boss, lover is thinking and adjust our behavior accordingly. While writing these words, for example, I am thinking about what you will be thinking when you read them, so that I can use the words that will make the most sense to you.

Imagine that you are at a cocktail party and a waiter comes by to offer you a shrimp canapé. You are already full, so you refuse politely. Your conversation partner, Lucy, who observes the exchange, will automatically engage in "theory of mind" to try to understand why you refused the canapé. Although she is attempting to uncover your motives, she will automatically use her own state to make inferences about yours. This instinctive strategy can work well, but it can also lead to the wrong conclusion. Because her own stomach is empty, Lucy is less likely to arrive at the true reason for your rejection of the pink amuse-bouche and more likely to assume that you believe the shrimp is bad or that you find it impolite to converse with your mouth full. When the waiter turns to her, she, too, declines with grace.

While the tendency to engage in theory of mind is useful—it helps us relate to one another and predict what people will do next—the human mind is not a perfect inference machine, and inevitably we will, at times, reach the wrong conclusions. The consequences can be greater than just passing on a hors d'oeuvre. Consider economic bubbles such as the one that collapsed the market in 2008. Financial bubbles occur when people trade in high volumes at prices that are unrealistic. There are many reasons why bubbles are generated, but it seems we would not have market bubbles if it weren't for theory of mind. Imagine that you are a trader playing the market. You sit in front of your computer watching trend lines do the tango, going up and down. You need to decide when to dance and when to retreat. Suddenly the numbers rise and rise, like a soufflé in a hot oven. "What is going on?" you think to yourself. "Why is everyone buying? What do they know that I don't?"

Neuroscientists Benedetto De Martino, Colin Camerer, and their colleagues at the California Institute of Technology have shown that traders who are most susceptible to bubbles, the ones who are most likely to buy at inflated prices, are also the ones who performed best on theory of mind tasks, such as guessing people's internal states simply by looking into their eyes.[22] In other words, economic decisions that create bubbles are more likely to be taken by people who give their partner the gift they really want for Valentine's Day. Why? A decision to ride the bubble happens when a trader believes that other people have positive information about the market. The trader thinks about what other people are thinking, and that process leaves him with the conclusion that there must be a valid reason for the rise. So he decides to buy at an inflated price.

* * *

There are two lessons to take away from all of this. First, we need to be careful when using other people's choices and actions to guide our own. Many times, influence happens under the radar, and all we can hope for is to become more aware—more aware that it is going on, more conscious that our inferences may be wrong, and more careful not to mindlessly trade our own unique tastes for those of another. In cases when we are consciously evaluating the opinions of others, such as looking up ratings on Yelp or Travelocity, we need to know that those ratings may not be as accurate as they seem. In the next chapter, I will consider how we can use others' opinions in a smarter way.

Second, if there is something we should learn from Mason, Livia, Harold, and the Adélie penguins, it is that one individual can make a difference. In fact, in describing the experiment Micah, Yadin, and I carried out, I failed to mention an important detail. The volunteers in our study would discard their own correct beliefs and adopt the false ones of others as long as everyone in the group, unanimously, supported the wrong answer. Yet if one other person gave the correct answer, the volunteers would stick to their original beliefs. In other words, even in a swarm, *one* divergent voice can cause others to act independently. You are influenced by others, but do not be fooled—others are also influenced by you. This is why your actions and choices matter not only for your own life but for the behavior of those around you.

8

⊰⊱

Is "Unanimous" as Reassuring as It Sounds? (Others, Part II)

How to Find Answers in an Unwise Crowd

"U nanimous" has a reassuring sound to it, don't you think? If the jury made a "unanimous" decision, we assume it was a straightforward case. And if "unanimous" is not an option, we will take the "majority" over the "minority" any day. A solution preferred by the "majority" instantly sounds better than one preferred by the "minority." Would you sign up with a physician favored by the majority or one favored by the minority? Exactly.

Marlon James, a celebrated Jamaican-born author, is accustomed to having his work judged unanimously by a group. In 2015, he was presented with the prestigious Man Booker Prize after a unanimous vote. The award committee dubbed his novel *A Brief History of Seven Killings* an extraordinary piece of work. With that prize, he joined the likes of Salman Rushdie, Ian McEwan, Iris Murdoch, and Kingsley Amis.

A decade earlier, when James submitted his debut novel, *John Crow's Devil*, for consideration, editors across the globe were also in complete agreement. They were unanimous in their assessment. There was one difference, though—back then they all agreed that James's work was not worth publishing. His manuscript was rejected no less than seventy-eight times. Given the eventual success of James's books, it is safe to say that those editors were wrong.

James recalled going to great lengths to destroy *John Crow's Devil* following the gazillion rejections. He took to heart, as one would, the opinion of so many professionals. "I even went on my friends' computers and erased it," he says.[1] Thankfully, he had a change of heart and rescued his deleted manuscript from cyberspace oblivion by searching his e-mail archives sometime later. His novel found a publishing home with lucky submission number 79.

James's story is not a rarity by any means. *Harry Potter and the Sorcerer's Stone* was rejected by twelve editors at different publishing houses, until finally, a year after it was first submitted for consideration, editor Barry Cunningham, at Bloomsbury Publishing, offered J. K. Rowling a £1,500 advance for her manuscript.[2]

Where Cunningham differed from the rest is that in making his decision, he received valuable advice from a unique avid reader: Alice Newton. Alice was eight years old at the time and the daughter of Bloomsbury's chairman, Nigel Newton. Mr. Newton gave Alice the first chapter of the Potter manuscript to read. She was instantly taken by the plot, devouring the pages and requesting more. He recalled her coming down from her room an hour later glowing, saying, "Dad, this is so much better than anything else."[3]

With that, Alice sealed J. K. Rowling's future, famously transforming her from a struggling single mother into a billionaire who went on to share her stories with millions of thankful kids around the globe.

When deciding to publish *Harry Potter*, Cunningham was likely aware that many editors had already rejected the manuscript. Yet he weighed the opinion of one little girl against those of a dozen experienced editors. As it turned out, he made the right decision. The rest of the editors were left to eat their hats.

The Real Reason for Crowd Wisdom

Cunningham succeeded by disregarding a prevalent notion—namely, that by tallying or averaging the opinions of many, you will make better choices. This notion famously dates back to Plymouth, England, in 1907. On a typical rainy day, crowds were drawn from all over the country to the annual Fat Stock and Poultry Exhibition, where a competition was held to see who could guess the weight of a chubby ox. Eight hundred people participated, writing down their estimates on small pieces of paper. The ox was then slaughtered and weighed. Lo and behold, when the cards were compiled, the median guess turned out to be 1,207 pounds—only 1 percent off from the ox's actual weight. The Victorian polymath Francis Galton went on to publish these findings in the prestigious journal *Nature*, concluding that the wisdom of the crowds is greater than originally thought.[4] His paper changed the way we make decisions.

A century later, the widely accepted view is that whether selecting a business strategy or a dinner menu, the more brains contributing to a decision, the merrier. The idea that the crowd is wise was popularized in recent years by James Surowiecki's famous book *The Wisdom of Crowds*.[5] If you read Surowiecki's book carefully, however, you will notice that below the title's surface, he cautions his readers that the group is wiser than the individual *only* under very specific conditions. Nevertheless, his readers, the media, and most of the world were left with the belief that, as a matter of principle, two brains are better than one, and a thousand brains are even better.

The truth, however, is not that simple. The group can be wise, but it can often be foolish. So why was the Plymouth crowd together able to estimate the weight of the ox better than a typical individual alone? As we are about to discover, the answer has very little to do with "wisdom."

Human Thermometers

The other day, while at work, I received a phone call from my children's babysitter, Lizbeth. Lizbeth informed me that my daughter, Livia, was not feeling well and she'd determined that Livia had a fever. Lizbeth, being the responsible caregiver she is, had taken my daughter's temperature not once, but twice, using two different thermometers. The first read 100.8 degrees and the second 100.4. Lizbeth concluded that the true temperature was approximately 100.6 degrees.

Why did Lizbeth bother to take the reading twice, using two devices? She'd correctly recognized that each thermometer can skew the reading one way or the other. No device is perfect—some have slight flaws in their design; others are old and overused. It is unlikely, however, that separate instruments from different manufacturers will have the exact same flaw and produce the same inaccuracies. If you average out the measurements, the errors can cancel each other out, giving a better reading. If I had had fifty thermometers lying around the house, Lizbeth would likely have obtained an even more accurate reading.

Imagine the Plymouth crowd as walking, talking thermometers. Each person takes a "reading" of the ox's weight, each making a

TRUTH

| Salma | Julianne | **=** | Charlie | Rosa |

MEAN

WEIGHT ⟶

Figure 8.1. *When people's guesses of the ox's weight bracketed the truth, the average guess was spot-on.*

unique error due to their distinct point of view, past experience, eyesight, and so on. Some, like Charlie and Rosa, slightly overestimate the weight of the ox while others, like Julianne and Salma, slightly underestimate it. People's estimates of the weight of the ox are imprecise. What is critical, though, is that they naturally distribute around the real weight of the ox—they *bracket* the truth. When that happens, the errors on either side of the truth cancel each other out, and so the average guess of a group of human thermometers is close to the true number.

It's not magic; nor is it wisdom. It's math. The problem, however, is that this principle works only under specific circumstances. The first condition that needs to be met is independence—the opinions of the people in the crowd need to be independent of one another. But are they?

Independence in an Interacting World

Every morning when Robert, a senior editor at a top publishing house, arrives at his office, he is greeted by a large pile of manuscripts from hopeful authors. His job is to sort through the stack on his desk and separate the potential Hemingways from the rest. It is a tricky job. Inevitably, at times Robert will enthusiastically assert that he has uncovered a golden egg only to discover after publication that no one is interested in his golden omelettes. Other times, he may pass on a manuscript that ends up being an international best seller. Robert, like everyone else in the publishing business, is intimately familiar with J. K. Rowling's multiple rejections, and it hangs above him like a dire warning.

Robert does not make his decisions alone; he has a team of seven colleagues who chip in to offer their views. That morning, he finds a potential winner: an intriguing nonfiction proposal on human behavior. He wants to bid on the proposal and needs to decide how much to offer as an advance. The specific amount is crucial. He has to figure out a number that will win him the bid in case other publishing houses make offers yet still allow the book to earn a profit.

He e-mails the book proposal to his team and sets up a meeting so that they can discuss it. He wants to know what everyone thinks—Jill, the junior editor; Sammy, who is in charge of marketing; Tamron, the head of finance; and the rest. Normally, he will walk into a meeting, briefly present the proposal, explain why he believes the book has potential, and elicit everyone's opinions. Yet something he has read in this particular proposal has made him change his mind. Unlike any other day, today he walks into the staff-filled room and says, "I want you each to take out a piece of paper and write down the amount you would offer for this manuscript." The members of the team comply, jotting down their answers on their notepads. Only then does Robert ask each member to share their number with everyone else and justify their assessment.

Robert is aware that his team of thermometers will be "wise" only if the assessment made by each of them is independent of the others'. If Robert had gone around the room, letting each member voice their opinion one at a time—a very common strategy—the team members would learn what others were thinking, and that information would bias their judgment. If the first member on Robert's team were to stand up and hugely endorse the book, the likelihood that the others would do so, too, even if they were not absolutely convinced before, would increase. That would be fine if the first person to give their answer happened to be right, but the strategy can be problematic otherwise. Imagine little Alice Newton sitting in a large boardroom listening to the high-flying editors voice their objections to Rowling's manuscript. There is a clear consensus: reject *Potter*! How likely is it that little Alice will say something different? What chance is there that she will stand up for Harry? What is the probability that she will even trust her own instincts? Very low. Even if Alice were an adult on equal terms with the others, research my colleagues and I conducted shows that in the face of apparent consensus, only about 30 percent of individuals will voice a different view.[6]

True independence, however, is almost impossible to construct. If prior to the staff meeting Jill, Sammy, and Tamron were chatting in the kitchen over coffee and creamy doughnuts, discussing the proposal, Jill's error in predicting the book's profit will no longer be independent of Sammy and Tamron's error. This is because if Sammy mentions that he thinks the book will be a best seller, Tamron, who initially underestimated the book's sales, will shift her belief toward that of charismatic Sammy. Their errors will now no longer cancel each other out; they no longer bracket the truth.

If you are planning to use crowd magic, you need to ask yourself to what extent the beliefs of the people on your team or social network are independent. If the individuals in your group had an opportunity to interact before expressing their opinions, their independence has been abolished.

Consider Facebook. Let's say it's Friday night and you plan to go to the cinema, but you are not sure what to see. You ask your Facebook friends for their advice. Ten people comment, and seven of them suggest *The Theory of Everything*. Did seven people like *The Theory of Everything* so much that the movie instantly came to mind when they commented on your post? Maybe. Here is another possibility: one friend recommended the movie on your wall and the others were then biased in that direction. Once a friend or two recommended the film, other friends who did not like the movie as much refrained from saying so, or even avoided recommending a different film so as not to offend the others or stand out as a black sheep.

Unlike thermometers, we are social creatures, and our default setting is to interact. Because society and people are so heavily intertwined, it is often impossible to elicit independent opinions from individuals. However, we can take certain actions to reduce that interdependence. Imagine you need to make a hiring decision and you ask four of your colleagues to interview a candidate. What you should do is ask all of them to send you their evaluations *before* discussing their assessment with one another, in order to enhance their independence. If you fail to do so, tallying many opinions will not necessarily make you wiser. It will, however, make you more confident. This is because self-assurance intensifies when people make interdependent decisions.[7] They think to themselves, "Hey, we all agree that this book will be a big hit, so we must be right." Maybe they are, or maybe they're in agreement because of social influence.

The Wise Crowd Within

In a universe parallel to our own, a terrible storm descended on Plymouth on the very day in 1907 of the Fat Stock and Poultry Exhibition. In truly British fashion, the exhibition committee decided to go ahead with the fair nonetheless. They would *keep calm and carry on*! A tent was put up to guard the animals from the rain and wind, and warm potato soup was prepared, to be offered free to visitors. Alas, despite these remarkable efforts, only one farmer, Jacob Wiseman, braved the storm to attend the fair. No matter, the organizers said, we will let the brave farmer guess the weight of the fat ox all on his own. Without the wisdom of crowds to rely on, what should Wiseman the farmer do?

To solve this problem, I am going to ask you to imagine Mr. Wiseman, the brave farmer, as a digital thermometer, the type you swipe across a child's forehead to get a reading. And I want you to imagine yourself as my daughter's dedicated babysitter, Lizbeth. Your task is to accurately measure my daughter's temperature using Mr. Wiseman. What should you do?

Well, what you should do is take Mr. Wiseman and swipe him across my daughter's forehead and read the result. Then you should do the same thing again and again, averaging your recordings to get the best measure. This is because Mr. Wiseman will give noisy readings. By "noisy," I do not mean acoustic cacophony. What I mean is that each reading will reflect the true temperature plus irrelevant factors. For example, maybe my daughter had a warm cup of milk immediately before the first time you took her temperature—making the number go up. Maybe you did not perform a full swipe on your second attempt, which made the number go down. On each reading, factors may skew the results one way or another, producing errors. Averaging multiple readings from one device will, on balance, give you a better guesstimate than just one reading.

The simple rules and statistics that make the group "wise" under the right circumstances also apply to a single mind. Mr. Wiseman needs to elicit the "wise crowd within his mind" to guess the weight of the fat ox. I am not implying that Mr. Wiseman has multiple personalities. But he does have multiple memories, multiple perspectives, and multiple beliefs. There is a lively crowd of eager farmers within him, and by asking himself the same question again and again, he may be able to tap into it.

The notion that we can use the "wise" crowd within a single mind was suggested by psychologists Ed Vul and Harold Pashler.[8] Ed and Harold created an online experiment where 428 individuals were asked the following trivia questions (jot down your own guesses on a piece of paper):

1. The area of the United States is what percentage of the area of the Pacific Ocean?
2. What percentage of the world's population lives in either China, India, or the European Union?
3. What percentage of the world's airports are in the United States?
4. What percentage of the world's roads are in India?
5. What percentage of the world's countries have a higher fertility rate than the United States?
6. What percentage of the world's telephone lines are in China, the United States, or the European Union?

7. Saudi Arabia consumes what percentage of the oil it produces?

8. What percentage of the world's countries have a higher life expectancy than the United States does?

Either a few minutes later or three weeks later, the same participants were asked the exact same questions again. If you want to try this out, take a fresh piece of paper and answer the questions a second time. Thereafter, take your first and second guesses and calculate your combined average answer on every question. Ed and Harold found that, on average, people's mean combined error was smaller than either their first or second error alone.* What's more, if people waited three weeks and only then answered the questions again, the effect was even more pronounced.

That means that if Robert the editor wants to minimize his mistakes when predicting a book's success over the course of his career, he is best advised to jot down his offer, sleep on it, and then jot down another figure a day, or even a week, later. The average of the two offers is the one he should use in a bid. Of course, it is often impossible to wait a few weeks or even twenty-four hours before making a decision. Robert may need to make a quick call. In those cases, he may still benefit from making two predictions closely in time and then combining them.

Why does this work? The answer, once again, is based on simple statistics. The reason you should ask yourself the same question a few times (preferably with some days in between), and then average your answers, is that you never use all the information

---

* I provide the answers to the questions in the Appendix at the end of this chapter, as well as instructions on how to calculate the average "combined" error, so that you can try this yourself. Your combined guess will not always be better; sometimes your first guess will be closer to the truth than your combined guess; sometimes your second will be more on the mark. Yet, on average, your mistakes will be smaller when you combine your guesses.

available to you when making a decision. Think about it like this: Robert has a lot of knowledge about the publishing world. He is familiar with the history of best sellers and flops; he can recall the good decisions he made in the past, as well as the bad; he has an understanding of why several of his past expectations did not materialize and why others did; he is aware of his audience, of trends, and of the competition. He will draw on this knowledge to make a decision.

But—and this is a very important *but*—he will never recall, or draw on, every single piece of information stored away in his brain. Some knowledge will be retrieved, and some will not. The process is partially random, but it can also be influenced by what Robert happened to experience that day. What that means is that the first time Robert considers a problem, some facts will come to mind and be integrated into his decision. The second time he considers a problem, some of the same facts will be used, some will not, and, importantly, some *new* facts will. Therefore, his second estimate will be slightly different from his first—he will be eliciting a different sample of information. If he combines his predictions together, he will be making a decision based on more data from within.

Ed and Harold found that if you ask yourself the above questions a second time, your combined answer will improve, on average, by 6.5 percent relative to your first guess. If you wait three weeks, you will be likely to do 16.5 percent better. That is a huge improvement. Waiting three weeks means your mind is fresh, you are less likely to remember what you thought a few weeks back, and you are more likely to come up with different reasons for your new guesses.* While your estimates will never be truly independent

---

* The authors made sure the participants did not look up the answers in the intermediate time.

of each other, decisions made three weeks apart are more independent than those made only a few minutes apart. So should Robert sack his team and vote on his own again and again to make a decision? Well, no. At least for the type of questions Ed and Harold asked, the average of two opinions elicited from the same person was only a third as good as the average of two opinions elicited from two independent people.

A Bias, Snowballing

Wisely, Robert decides to keep his team on the payroll and consult them when making a choice. But once the independent opinions have been gathered, how should he combine them to reach a decision? Contrary to the classic fat ox example, simply counting votes and determining the median or averaging everyone's opinions will not always be the optimal solution.[9] We've already witnessed as much in the cases of *Harry Potter* and Marlon James. The problem is not only that people's estimates can be interdependent but also that they can be systematically biased.

For example, if the fat ox is standing next to a skinny ox, most people will overestimate how fat the fat ox really is. This is because our brains perceive everything in a relative manner; next to a skinny ox, the fat ox looks even fatter. In this case, people's errors will not distribute around the true weight of the ox but, rather, will be shifted in one direction. So in circumstances where there is good reason to believe that people are biased, systematically wrong, or interdependent, we should be wary of the so-called wisdom of crowds.*

Instances in which the majority tends to err in the same direc-

---

* In such cases, the "wise crowd within" principle—that is, considering several guesses from just one source—will not work, either.

Figure 8.2. *When a fat ox stands next to a skinny ox, he seems even larger. This biased perception is shared by all, making the average guess of the crowd larger than the true weight of the ox.*

tion are endless. These include errors in predicting the future: people tend to be overly optimistic—for example, underestimating how long projects will take to complete and how much they will cost.[10] They also extend to trivia questions—for instance, when asked to name the capital of Brazil, most people will assume it is Rio de Janeiro, but in fact it is Brasilia. And these errors encompass perceptual illusions, too. The human brain produces many systematic biases. Because most people's brains are wired in a similar manner, we tend to fail in the same places. Obviously, in such cases, averaging opinions or counting votes will get us nowhere.

In fact, there is a danger that in a group setting biases will expand, snowballing to huge proportions. Let's take a look at an intriguing example of how this may happen.

The data on the next page link the personality trait "watchfulness" of fifteen CEOs and the CEO's company's annual profit in millions of dollars. "Watchfulness" was measured using the Draler International Watchfulness Scale (DIWS); scores can range from −20 to 20.

CEO's DIWS Score	Annual Profit (in million $)
4	6
5	15
–6	26
7	39
3	–1
12	134
15	215
22	474
8	54
6	26
–8	54
12	134
18	314
–3	–1
–10	90

I am going to ask you to use the above data to predict the annual profit of five other companies whose CEOs have the following DIWS scores: 10, 0, 19, –17, –1.

If you are like most people, your numbers will indicate that you assume that the relationship between a CEO's DIWS score and the company's annual profit is more positively linear than it really is. When humans infer the relationship between any two variables— be it the relationship between the size of a tomato and its sweetness or between office temperature and the number of colleagues' interactions—they are biased. They see positive linear relationships even when there are none.[11] This means that we are likely to conclude that as one variable increases (let's say, the size of a tomato), the other will increase in similar proportion (the sweetness of the tomato).

Okay, fine: we tend to see positive relationships even when they do not exist. Here is the interesting part, though: imagine you are an HR consultant and you are advising companies on whom to hire as a CEO. You use the CEO's "watchfulness" score to predict expected annual profit under each candidate's leadership and submit your biased predictions to your boss. Your boss sees your predictions, and his mind concludes that if a CEO is high on "watchfulness," his company is likely to pull in a higher profit. He uses this new rule to make predictions about other companies, which he sends to a group of analysts. Even if there was no relationship at all between a company's profit and a CEO's DIWS score, by the time data and knowledge have been transferred between four or more people, the inherent biases will have overcome the true evidence.[12]

By the way: if you are wondering what makes someone high on "watchfulness," I have no idea—I made this trait up, and DIWS does not exist.

These types of experiments have been conducted in the lab.[13] They clearly show that even if two variables are negatively related to each other (this means that as one variable increases, the other decreases) or are related to each other in a nonlinear fashion (this means that as one variable increases, the other does not increase or decrease in proportion), after enough people convey the relationship to others, a positive relationship is assumed. So you can see how even subtle biases of the mind can snowball, becoming stronger and larger when humans interact.

The product of two phenomena that are integral to the human brain can result in not-so-wise crowds. The first phenomenon is the well-documented tendency of our brains to produce unconscious biases. From cognitive biases to errors in decision-making and forecasts, the human brain has evolved for greatness but has preserved countless biases.

| data | Learner 1 | Learner 2 | Learner 3 | Learner 4 | Learner 5 | Learner 6 | Learner 7 | Learner 8 | Learner 9 |

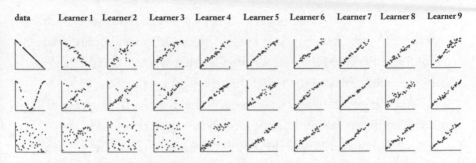

Figure 8.3. *Biases snowballing. The leftmost panel in each row is the data that was seen by the first learner. The subsequent columns show the data produced by successive generations of learners, each one trained with the data from the previous learner. Each row represents a single sequence of nine learners. The patterns reveal that learners are biased to perceive positive linear relationships, regardless of the initial data.*[14]

The second is the human inclination for social learning. If by nature we look to others for information and clues about what is true and, like any humans, these individuals we consult carry inherent biases, it is inevitable that falsehoods will sometimes increase when individuals come together, creating expanding bubbles that will eventually burst. Such snowballing biases are by no means confined to large groups, such as financial markets or online networks. False beliefs can also develop and expand among friends and family members (false memories shared by siblings for years), business partners (optimistic expectations go wild when two enthusiasts meet), and cultural groups (the idea that *our* group is intrinsically superior).

The Equality Heuristic

Our hefty reliance on the opinion of the majority can therefore translate to suboptimal choices, odd beliefs, and missed opportunities. There are numerous examples of ideas that were once accepted by the majority, in a specific time and place, but are now considered false—for example, the idea that women are not fit for higher education and the belief that the world is flat.

Yet our gut often tells us to go with the majority. It is operating off a "heuristic," a simple, easy, effortless way to make decisions—a mental shortcut. While this heuristic can help us at times, it can also lead us astray. My colleague Bahador Bahrami, who studies group decision-making at University College London, calls this tendency the "equality bias." What he is referring to is the idea that when making decisions, we often revert to an easy strategy of weighing everyone's opinion equally, regardless of differences in people's reliability and expertise. This is true not only in countries where democracy has been the norm for generations, like the United States and Denmark; Bahador and his colleagues tested citizens of China and Iraq, and there, too, he found that people use a rule of thumb when making decisions: they go with the popular vote.

The problem is that, in many instances, people are simply not equal in their skills and knowledge. If you need to make a medical decision, it's reasonable to put more weight on the opinion of a doctor with a medical degree from Johns Hopkins University than on that of your well-intentioned uncle. Unless, of course, your sympathetic uncle also has a medical degree from a good university, in which case weighing both equally is probably the logical thing to do.

Still, Bahador found that people often ignore information that can help them determine who the expert in the room is. Instead, they prefer to give everyone's opinion equal weight; it just feels right and does not require much cognitive effort. This tendency comes at a cost: by weighing everyone's opinion equally, rather than according to expertise, people in Bahador's experiments made many wrong decisions.[15]

All of this may sound rather bleak, especially considering how often we are exposed to the opinions of individuals online, most of whom we know nothing about—thus we are unable to tease the identities apart and separate the experts from the rest. That being said, it would be surprising if the access we now have to the opinions of so many people turns out to be utterly useless. The key, I believe, is to use this resource thoughtfully, rather than blindly. In the haystack that is the crowd, is there a way to identify wisdom?

Figure 8.4. Others. *Beware of the equality bias—weigh people's opinions according to their expertise on the topic.* Our instinct is to go with the majority vote. The majority, however, can be wrong. Instead of giving everyone's opinion equal weight, consider information that can help determine who the expert in the room is. It just might be an eight-year-old girl.

The Surprisingly Popular Vote

Take a moment to answer the following questions:

1. What is the capital of Pennsylvania?
2. If it takes five machines five minutes to make five widgets, how long does it take one hundred machines to make one hundred widgets?
3. In a lake, there is a patch of lily pads. Every day, the patch doubles in size. If it takes forty-eight days for the patch to cover the entire lake, how long would it take for the patch to cover half of the lake?

Before reading the answers below, do one more thing: look at the questions again, only now guess how *most* people would answer them.

The majority say that Philadelphia is the capital of Pennsylvania, that it will take one hundred machines one hundred minutes to make one hundred widgets, and that the patch will cover half the lake in twenty-four days. These are intuitive answers, given by approximately 83 percent of the population. They are wrong.

In fact, Harrisburg is the capital of Pennsylvania, one hundred machines would make one hundred widgets in five minutes (if it takes five machines five minutes to make five widgets, that means one machine can make one widget in five minutes, so one hundred machines could make one hundred widgets in the same amount of time), and it would take the patch forty-seven days to cover half the lake (on day forty-eight the patch will double, therefore covering the whole lake).

Imagine that I had not revealed the answers and you were still trying to figure them out. What would you do? How would you uncover the correct answers? Obviously, relying on the majority vote in this case will not give you the correct answer. For the last two questions, you might want to ask a friend who is a "number person," maybe someone working in finance or an engineer. That seems sensible. The problem, however, is that even those who use math and statistics for a living often provide wrong answers to these questions. Shane Frederick, a professor at Yale who came up with these questions, went out and asked six hundred finance professionals to take this short quiz. Only 40 percent got a perfect score.[16] Even among MIT students—a cohort that includes some of the most technically skilled minds in the world—half gave the wrong answers. I am sure that most of these students could figure out the correct answers if they paused to consider the questions carefully. However, half were fooled by hasty intuition.

John McCoy is one of those MIT students who gave the right answers. Yet to do so, he did not even bother reading the questions. Rather, he used a trick called "the surprising popular vote," a technique anyone can use to find the truth with the help of the crowd. The method was developed together with his adviser, the behavioral economist Drazen Prelec.[17] It works like this:

First, John tallied up everyone's answers. Let's take the widget question as an example. For that question, approximately 80 percent of those surveyed said it would take one hundred minutes (wrong answer), and 20 percent said five minutes (right answer). Instead of going with the popular (and wrong) vote, he next tallied up what people predicted others would say. Most people realized that the majority of individuals would think the answer was one hundred minutes for one hundred machines to make one hundred widgets. This is true whether they themselves knew the correct answer or not. So say about 96 percent of individuals predicted that most people would think the answer is one hundred and maybe 4 percent said that most people would think it would take five minutes for one hundred machines to make one hundred widgets. Finally, John looked for the answer that was *more popular than people expected.* In this case, it was five minutes: 20 percent of individuals said five minutes, but only 4 percent believed that others would say five minutes—this answer was *surprisingly more popular than predicted.*

John and Drazen showed that this technique works not only for "trick" questions like the above but also for questions in which the majority is right, such as "What is the capital of South Carolina?" They found that the method also works for a range of other problems, such as identifying the best move in chess, providing medical diagnoses and artistic judgments, and even for forecasting political and economic events. All these problems, John and Drazen found, were best solved by the crowd when employing the rule of *the surprisingly popular vote.*

The technique is aimed at uncovering "inside knowledge." It does, however, require that at least one soul know the truth (otherwise there will be no correct vote—surprisingly popular or otherwise), but it does not require the crowds to be experts—novices will do. While you might turn to MIT students to help you solve a math problem, you would probably not survey them for their opinions about art, right? Well, when John employed the *surprisingly popular vote,* he found that MIT students did as well as art gallery owners in determining the market price of a piece of art. On average, the MIT students were off the mark, but the *surprisingly popular vote* was spot-on.

* * *

When sampling, tallying, and eliciting opinions, we need to remember to pause; we must assess the likelihood that people's opinions are interdependent and biased, and consider whether they should, in fact, be weighted *unequally*. In some sense, the crowd does encompass wisdom. But it is not unusual for that wisdom to be held by a minority—by the seventy-ninth editor evaluating Marlon James's manuscript, by an eight-year-old girl reading *Harry Potter*, by the 17 percent of the population that thoroughly worked through a tricky math problem. Whenever you are gathering opinions online or offline, and whether you are doing so to make a choice in your personal life, a purchasing decision, or to arrive at a professional verdict—be careful. Your "gut" may direct you toward the majority, but keep in mind that even in our world of ratings and reviews, tallying and averaging many views can lead to suboptimal solutions.

APPENDIX

Answers to Vul and Pashler's questions:

1. 6.3
2. 44.4
3. 30.3
4. 10.5
5. 58
6. 72.4
7. 18.9
8. 20.3

INSTRUCTIONS

For each of the eight questions, take your first answer and subtract it from the correct answer above. The difference is your error for each question. Square each error (this will get rid of any negative numbers) so that it reflects absolute error and not the direction of the error. Then average all your square errors across the eight questions (this is the averaged square error for your first answers). Then do the exact same thing for your second set of answers (this is the averaged square error for your second answers). Finally, take your first and second answers for each of the eight questions and average those. This is your mean answer for each question. Take all eight mean answers and calculate your average square errors as above. Is this number smaller than the averaged square error for your first answers? Is it also smaller than the averaged square error for your second answers?

9

⟨⟨⟩⟩

The Future of Influence?

Your Mind in My Body

Just like us, the first humans were social creatures. They lived together, moved together, and, inevitably, influenced one another. They had yet to evolve language, but they could communicate fear, excitement, and love with facial expressions, touch, and sound. The danger of a nearby predator could be expressed with a sudden scream, signaling others to run away. The joy of human interaction could be expressed with laughter, signaling others to move closer.

Then our ancestors began to talk. When exactly this occurred is a mystery. Unlike written language, verbal language leaves no physical trace. Experts estimate that language first emerged anywhere between 1.75 million years ago,[1] around the time our ancestors invented tools, and 50,000 years ago,[2] which is about when "modern humans" appeared on Earth. With language, the ability for sharing opinions, beliefs, and desires expanded tremendously.

If the earlier estimates are accurate, than perhaps our ancestors debated whether or not to leave Africa and explore the rest of the world. Maybe they, too, were persuaded by a Kennedy-like figure to reach beyond their immediate environment.

And then writing emerged. Written language (rather than just numbers) appeared about 5,200 years ago.[3] Once again, the ability to propagate knowledge reached a new level. No longer would you have to directly interact with another human being at a certain time and place to share your ideas. Now you were able to affect those you would never meet—people who would exist after you and those who were miles away. In fact, the greatest source of influence on human beliefs *today* may be a collection of prose written more than two thousand years ago.

Written language was followed by the ability to print. This technological advance took place around the year 1440 and, as a result, opinions could be transmitted to large masses of people around the globe.[4] Print was followed by radio in the beginning of the twentieth century.[5] Radio introduced the ability to instantly transmit speech to people far away. Around 1927, radio was followed by television,[6] though TV was not available to the masses until the 1950s.[7] This development meant that images and expressions, in addition to just voices, could be shared. While many were on the receiving end of these technologies, only a minority had the opportunity to transport *their* ideas to others.

Then, around 1990, the Internet emerged.[8] The World Wide Web meant that sharing, affecting, and influencing became free for all. People could express their opinions to the world using words, images, and sounds.

In the last few thousand years of accelerating technology and rapidly changing environments, one entity did not alter much. That structure was the target of these technologies—the human brain. Evolution is slower than technology, and the principle organization of the brain has not experienced significant change since written language first appeared.[9] True, if we look further back and compare ourselves to the very first humans, some important modifications are apparent, particularly within our frontal lobes.[10] However, even in comparison to these first humans, our brains are more like theirs than different. Many of the desires, motivations, and fears that shaped their beliefs and actions shape ours today, and the basic biological principles of how one mind affects another remain.

Two Brains and a Wire

If you make a sound, a movement, or type a word, you are generating a signal that can be picked up by other brains. In essence, you are connecting your brain with another's via sound, sight, and touch. Every word you utter was once an electrical signal in your brain that was eventually transformed into a sound, which could be picked up by receptors in another person's ear, then converted into electrical signals in that person's brain and interpreted as a word, a sentence, an idea.[11] And so here is an idea, one I am about to transfer to you via written language. Can we connect our brains directly without the need to make a change in the environment first? Could an electrical signal in my brain be converted into an electrical signal in yours, changing your behavior and thoughts, without me needing to first write a word or make a sound? If the answer is yes, this suggests that influence can be stripped down to neuronal firing in one brain altering neural firing in another.

In the last few years, neuroscientists have shown that you can physically connect two brains so that one brain learns directly from the electrical signals generated by the other. Until recently, this sounded like science fiction—a buzzing wire transferring knowledge from one brain to the next—but it is happening now in respectable laboratories at universities around the world.

Before I share these interesting studies with you, I need to make something clear. We are at least as far away from directly transmitting abstract ideas between two brains as we were from landing a man on the moon when John F. Kennedy made his famous speech. However, some scientists believe that we are at the *Sputnik* stage, making initial strides in that direction. Let's explore those first steps in transmitting signals directly from one brain to another without the need to speak or gesture.

I will start with the transmission of simple signals between the brains of two rats. Lab rats will work hard to receive rewards, like sugar water or a piece of cheese. If one rat figures out how to get such rewards, another rat may learn from it by observation. Could such knowledge also be directly transferred from one rat brain to another?

Apparently, yes. At a laboratory at Duke University, a rat—I'll call him Einstein—was trained to receive water by following a relatively simple rule: when a green light flashed, Einstein had to press the lever to his right; when a red light flashed, he had to press the lever to his left. Einstein was an Ivy League rat, so he caught on fast. Next, an electrode was inserted into Einstein's brain so that electrical signals could be recorded. The electrode was then connected to a computer, which was then connected to another rat's brain, transmitting signals. I'll call the second rat Homer. Homer, too, had to press the right or left lever at the correct moment to receive water, but he, unlike Einstein, could not see the red or green lights. The only information available to Homer was the electrical signals transmitted directly to his brain from Einstein. Homer

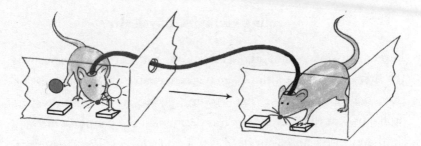

Figure 9.1. *Einstein the rat influences Homer the rat by sending signals directly from his brain to Homer's. As a result, Homer learns from Einstein how to solve a problem to gain more rewards.*

then had to figure out which lever to press by interpreting those signals.

It took Homer some time, but after forty-five hours of playing this game (with lots of breaks in between) he had a eureka moment: "Hey, the answer is in my head!" Seven out of ten times, Homer got the answer right and was rewarded with a large sip of cool, refreshing water.[12] Just as teachers get a bonus when their students do well, every time Homer got the answer right, Einstein received bonus water, which motivated him to send out an even clearer signal to Homer. To really drive their point home, the Duke scientists showed that transmitting data from Einstein to Homer can be accomplished across continents via the Internet. While Einstein was pressing levers in North Carolina, Homer was receiving electrical signals in Brazil.[13]

Einstein influenced Homer, and he did it without Homer ever having laid eyes on Einstein, without Homer ever hearing a sound from Einstein's mouth. It was the bare essentials of communication that caused a reaction—a firing cell in one brain altering the firing of cells in another brain. This, in turn, led to a change in behavior.

Connecting Humans, Physically?

Direct transmission of signals from one rat brain to another was the first step, but the ultimate goal was to enable direct transmission from one human to another. Adding people to the mix presents problems, not the least of which is permission to open up someone's skull and insert an electrode. Even if you find a willing volunteer, the institutional ethics review board is unlikely to allow it.

In the summer of 2014, one neurologist decided not to wait for such approval. He boarded a plane to Belize and paid a local neurosurgeon named Joel Cervantes $30,000 to cut open his brain and insert a small device that would allow him to conduct research on himself. His name was Kennedy—Phil Kennedy.[14]

Fifteen years earlier, Phil Kennedy had performed a similar procedure on the brain of a paralyzed man. The procedure allowed the otherwise locked-in patient to govern a computer cursor with his thoughts alone, so that he could communicate with the outside world. For legal, practical, and funding reasons, Kennedy was unable to perform the procedure again in the United States. Nor was he able to find another patient to volunteer. A stubborn man, Kennedy was unwilling to give up on his goal. And so he found himself on the operating table in Belize in 2014. For a while following the surgery, Kennedy was able to record neural firing from his own living, thinking brain. However, his surgery and recovery were not without complications, and he had to remove the device from his head before he was able to achieve a significant scientific breakthrough.[15]

As a result of such practical and ethical problems, noninvasive methods, instead of invasive ones, are often utilized to record and transmit signals between human brains. One solution involves electroencephalography (EEG), a relatively simple technique in which multiple electrodes are used to record electrical signals across the scalp rather than through the scalp. These signals can be input to a computer and transmitted to another person or animal. For example, at Harvard University, brain signals were recorded from a human brain and transmitted to a rat's brain.[16] This exercise is actually more valuable than it may sound. One of the ultimate goals of a human-rat interface is to develop little "fighter rats," whose movements are controlled by human thought, so that they, for instance, can navigate into enemy territories.[17] With this goal in mind (no pun intended), the group of researchers at Harvard set out to show that a person's thoughts could control the movement of a rat's tail.

They asked a human volunteer to sit in front of a computer and flashed squares and circles on the screen while recording signals from the volunteer's scalp using an EEG. The signals elicited from your brain when you look at a circle are slightly different from the signals elicited when you look at a square. Those signals were input to a computer and then transmitted to a rat's brain via ultrasound. The ultrasound triggered neural activity in a particular region of the rat's brain. Whenever the human saw a circle, this

Figure 9.2. *Human brain moving rat's tail.*[18]

signal would activate neurons in the rat's brain that made its tail go up, and whenever the human saw a square, the signal would activate other neurons that made its tail go down. There is nothing special about circles and squares; you could use images of unicorns and burgers if you prefer. In fact, just thinking of unicorns and burgers can suffice.

The technique is similar in principle to what is known as BCI (brain-computer interface). BCI is a method that has helped patients who, for example, have lost the use of a limb. Take Jan Scheuermann. In 1996, Jan was diagnosed with spinocerebellar ataxia, a genetic neurodegenerative disorder, and soon after lost the ability to move any of her limbs. Unable to walk, feed, or dress herself, Jan was entirely dependent on her caregivers.[19] In 2012, her doctor suggested a radical solution that seemed too bizarre to be true: the introduction of a robotic limb that she would control by her thoughts alone.

It sounded a bit futuristic, but Jan gave it a go. The procedure required surgery, during which two quarter-inch-square electrode grids were implanted in her brain. The electrodes recorded the signals from Jan's neurons when she thought about moving her arm. Those electric currents were then transmitted to a robot and signaled the robot's arm to move. Merely two weeks following surgery, Jan was able to move her new arm, and shortly after, she was feeding herself.

Jan was an ambitious woman, and so after a few years she decided she wanted to do more, much more. Her new goal was to fly a fighter jet—with her brain. Only three years after the implant, Jan was perfectly controlling an F-35 and a single-engine Cessna in a flight simulator as part of a DARPA (Defense Advanced Research Projects Agency) project. In the words of DARPA director Arati Prabhakar, "We can now see the future where we can free the brain from the limitations of the human body."[20]

If we can move a robotic arm with our thoughts, can we move another person's hand with our minds, too? Indeed, after rat-to-rat transmission, human-to-rat transmission, and human-to-machine transmission came a demonstration of human-to-human transmission. Here, again, EEG was used to record signals from a volunteer—this time, while the volunteer thought about moving his hand. This signal was then transferred to a computer and transmitted across the Internet. Once it arrived at its destination, it was converted into a magnetic signal (see figure 9.3). Small magnetic pulses were then transmitted to a second person through his scalp with a machine called TMS (transcranial magnetic stimulation). These magnetic pulses triggered a neural reaction, and voilà—the person's finger instantaneously moved, without the person consciously desiring it.[21]

What we can learn from Einstein teaching Homer which button to press via wires connecting their brains, and from a man moving another's finger with his thoughts, is that changing behav-

Figure 9.3. *The person on the left is using his thoughts to move the other person's finger (Credit: The University of Washington).*[22]

ior is about altering the pattern of neural firing inside a person's brain. But if we find a way to influence brain activity directly, are we inherently changing the mind? And will we one day be able to alter opinions and beliefs by connecting brains?

Your Mind in My Body?

Emotions were running high at the London School of Economics on a Monday night. Blood was rushing to the faces of the speakers on the stage; audience members were raising their voices; and less than polite expressions were uttered by all. If I asked you, you would probably guess that the topic of discussion at the full-capacity auditorium was the state of unemployment, or inequality, or the upcoming elections. You would be wrong. The question working up hundreds of people was "What can the brain tell us about the mind?"

Next to me on the panel sat an emeritus Oxford professor of philosophy. He had spent the previous twenty minutes using the word "nonsense" to describe the work of the greatest neuroscientists of our time, including two Nobel Prize laureates. When it was my turn to talk, I said something like "I am interested in how the brain computes the value of the options in front of us." That seemed like a noncontroversial statement to me. I was very much mistaken. The philosophy professor jumped out of his seat and pointed his finger in my direction. "But it is not your brain that is computing the options! It is *you* who is computing the options." "But I am my brain," I replied. "No, you are not," he insisted. "You are your arms and your legs—all of it is you."

That is true: I am my arms, my legs, my lungs, my heart, *and* my brain. It is also true that if you affect any of my other organs, you will consequently be affecting my brain. Punch me in the arm and my brain will signal the pain; put ice on my leg and my brain will create the feeling of cold; insert a knife into my heart and my brain will eventually stop functioning altogether. The reverse also holds: alter the function of my brain and you can change the function of my body parts—the brain controls all of them.

Yet if you chop off my legs, I will still, essentially, be me. If you transplant the professor emeritus's heart into my body, I will still, very much, be me. With his heart in my body, I would still have a strong preference for crumpets with cream cheese and smoked salmon, a love for running, and a passion for understanding human behavior. If, however, you transplanted the philosopher's brain into my body, I would find myself wearing a plaid jacket and speaking in a posh English accent. I would not be able to recognize my children and would have very different ideas of what makes me essentially me.

Brain tumors, head injuries, and chemical substances that find their way into your brain can dramatically change who you are. Physical injuries to your brain can completely alter your thoughts, feelings, memories, and personality. For example, surgically remove your hippocampi and you will be unable to create new memories of your life,[23] or insert a large metal rod through your frontal lobes and you will become implosive and antisocial.[24] Your brain creates your mind, and so changing your brain will change your mind.

Maybe one day we will affect each other's actions and thoughts by directly altering neural activity in each other's brains. Just as neurons in my brain affect other neurons in my brain—altering *my* memories, values, and actions—they could directly alter the firing of neurons in your brain—changing *your* memories, values, and actions. Thoughts, like the idea of conquering the moon or giving introverts a voice, are, in essence, electrical-chemical signals in our brains. These signals can be recorded, they can be transmitted, and they can be interpreted, and so it may in principle be possible to affect each other's thoughts in this way. Of course, for that to happen, we'll need a much more precise understanding of the complex circuitry of neurons in the human brain and how their function maps onto thoughts and behavior. This understanding, if possible, is far in the future.

* * *

While you may not yet be altering another person's brain activity directly, you are nonetheless altering it. You are simply using language, expressions, and actions to do so. A deeper understanding of how the mind and brain function can therefore help us in creating impact and avoiding systematic errors when trying to change others. Many of our instincts about influence—from insisting the other is wrong to attempting to exert control—are ineffective because they are incompatible with how the mind and brain operate.

An attempt to change will be successful if it is well matched with the core elements that govern the working of our brains. The aim of this book was to map out these factors—priors, emotion, incentives, agency, curiosity, state, and other people—and how they affect us. Biological principles, behavioral rules, and psychological theories can be hard to remember. But stories, plots, and characters stick in your mind; they provide a vivid emotional tale that you can make sense of and retrieve easily. The next time you encounter a sign saying, "Employees must wash their hands," remember that immediate rewards work better than threats for motivating people to act. The next time you water your plants, remember that offering control is a stronger tool for influence than giving orders. The next time you listen to a preflight safety brief-

ing, recall the power of reframing a message to highlight the possibility of progress, rather than doom, for getting people to pay
attention. My hope is that the characters in this book and the
stories they tell will live happily at the back of your mind, raising
their heads every so often when the time is right.

APPENDIX

—◦◦◦—

The Influential Brain

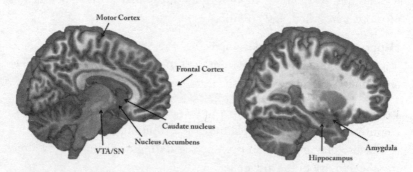

The Machinery of the Mind *Displayed are sagittal slices of the brain. This is what the inside of our brain looks like if we were to cut through the brain from the top of our head down to our neck. The left slice is a cut close to the middle of our head, and the right slice is a cut about halfway from the middle of the head and the side of the head. Highlighted are some of the key regions that form the neural networks discussed in the book. (Figure courtesy of Caroline Charpentier)*

The human brain consists of interconnected regions, which together produce actions, thoughts, and beliefs. Affecting one node in a system of connected regions will alter other nodes, changing what people do and what they believe in. These are some of the key regions discussed in the book:

Ventral tegmental area/substantia nigra (VTA/SN): These structures in the midbrain house dopaminergic neurons, which signal expectations of rewards. The neurons activate more when we receive an unexpected reward and fire less when a reward is unexpectedly denied. Neurons here project to parts of the striatum (among other regions), a structure deep in the brain.

Nucleus accumbens: The nucleus accumbens is part of the striatum and receives signals from dopaminergic neurons in the VTA/SN (among other regions). The region is sometimes referred to as the reward center of the brain, as it is critical for signaling the anticipation of rewards.

Amygdala: The amygdala is important for processing and signaling emotion and arousal. It has connections with a vast number of other regions, and that allows emotion to modulate many functions, such as memory, perception, and attention.

Hippocampus: The hippocampus, in the medial temporal lobe, is important for memory. It sits right next to the amygdala, which allows emotion to significantly alter our recollections.

Frontal cortex: Regions in the frontal cortex are important for higher cognitive functions such as planning and thinking. Parts of the frontal cortex also play an important role in regulating our emotions by altering the activity in the amygdala.

Motor cortex: The motor cortex is important for inducing action. It also receives signals that originate in the VTA/SN and signals from the striatum.

Notes

—◇◇◇—

Prologue

1. "CNN Reagan Library Debate: Later Debate Full Transcript," September 16, 2015, http://cnnpressroom.blogs.cnn.com/2015/09/16/cnn-reagan-lib rary-debate-later-debate-full-transcript/.
2. Diana I. Tamir and Jason P. Mitchell, "Disclosing Information About the Self Is Intrinsically Rewarding," *Proceedings of the National Academy of Sciences* 109, no. 21 (2012).
3. https://en.wikipedia.org/wiki/Climate_change_opinion_by_country.

1. (Priors) Does Evidence Change Beliefs?

1. See E. Berscheid, K. Dion, E. Hatfield, and G. W. Walster, "Physical Attractiveness and Dating Choice: A Test of the Matching Hypothesis," *Journal of Experimental Social Psychology* 7 (1971): 173–89; T. Bouchard Jr. and M. McGue, "Familial Studies of Intelligence: A Review," *Science* 212 (May 29, 1981): 1055–59; D. M. Buss, "Human Mate Selection," *American Scientist* 73 (1985): 47–51; S. G. Vandenberg, "Assortative Mating, or Who Marries Whom?," *Behavior Genetics* 11 (1972): 1–21.

2. Martha McKenzie-Minifie, "Where Would You Live in Europe?," *EUobserver,* December 2014.

3. internetstatslive.com.

4. Charles G. Lord, Lee Ross, and Mark R. Lepper. "Biased Assimilation and Attitude Polarization: The Effects of Prior Theories on Subsequently Considered Evidence," *Journal of Personality and Social Psychology* 37, no. 11 (November 1979): 2098–2109.

5. J. W. McHoskey, "Case Closed? On the John F. Kennedy Assassination: Biased Assimilation of Evidence and Attitude Polarization," *Basic and Applied Social Psychology* 1 (1985): 395–409; G. D. Munro, S. P. Leary, and T. P. Lasane, "Between a Rock and a Hard Place: Biased Assimilation of Scientific Information in the Face of Commitment," *North American Journal of Psychology* 6 (2004): 431–44; Guy A. Boysen, and David L. Vogel, "Biased Assimilation and Attitude Polarization in Response to Learning About Biological Explanations of Homosexuality," *Sex Roles* 57, nos. 9–10 (2007): 755–62.

6. Cass R. Sunstein, S. Bobadilla-Suarez, S. Lazzaro, and Tali Sharot, "How People Update Beliefs About Climate Change: Good News and Bad News," *Cornell Law Review* (forthcoming); Tali Sharot and Cass R. Sunstein, "Why Facts Don't Unify Us," *New York Times*, September 2, 2016.

7. Sharot and Sunstein, "Why Facts Don't Unify Us."

8. Albert Henry Smyth, *The Writings of Benjamin Franklin*, vol. 10, *1789–1790* (New York: Macmillan, 1907), p. 69; Daniel Defoe, *The Political History of the Devil* (Joseph Fisher, 1739).

9. Amy Hollyfield, "For True Disbelievers, the Facts Are Just Not Enough," *St. Petersburg Times,* June 29, 2008.

10. Opinion poll carried out for Daily Kos by Research 2000, July 2009.

11. NBC News, 2010.

12. Dave Asprey, "Dave Asprey Recipe: How to Make Bulletproof Coffee . . . and Make Your Morning Bulletproof Too," Bulletproof, 2010, https://www.bulletproofexec.com.

13. Kris Gunnars, "Three Reasons Why Bulletproof Coffee Is a Bad Idea," Authority Nutrition, https://authoritynutrition.com/3-reasons-why-bulletproof-coffee-is-a-bad-idea/.

14. Danny Sullivan, "Google Now Notifies of 'Search Customization' and Gives Searchers Control," 2008, http://searchengineland.com/google-now-notifies-of-search-customization-gives-searchers-control-14485.

15. Ibid.

16. Peter C. Wason, "On the Failure to Eliminate Hypotheses in a Conceptual Task," *Quarterly Journal of Experimental Psychology*, 12, no. 3 (1960): 129–40.

17. D. M. Kahan, E. Peters, E. C. Dawson, and P. Slovic, "Motivated Numeracy and Enlightened Self-Government," Yale Law School, Public Law Working Paper, no. 307 (2013).

18. Hugo Mercier and Dan Sperber, "Why Do Humans Reason? Arguments for an Argumentative Theory," *Behavioral and Brain Sciences* 34, no. 2 (2011): 57–74.

19. Andreas Kappes, Read Montague, Ann Harvey, Terry Lohrenz, and Tali Sharot, "Motivational Blindness in Financial Decision-Making," 2014 annual meeting of the Society for Neuroeconomics, Miami, FL.

20. Sarah Rudorf, Bernd Weber, and Camelia M. Kuhnen, "Stock Ownership and Learning from Financial Information," 2014 annual meeting of the Society for Neuroeconomics, Miami, FL.

21. A. J. Wakefield, S. H. Murch, A. Anthony, et al., "Retracted: Ileal-Lymphoid-Nodular Hyperplasia, Non-Specific Colitis, and Pervasive Developmental Disorder in Children, *Lancet* 351, no. 9103 (1998): 637–41.

22. Susan Dominus, "The Crash and Burn of an Autism Guru," *New York Times*, April 20, 2011.

23. F. Godlee, J. Smith, and H. Marcovitch, "Wakefield's Article Linking MMR Vaccine and Autism Was Fraudulent," *BMJ* 342 (2011): C7452.

24. Z. Horne, D. Powell, J. E. Hummel, and K. J. Holyoak, "Countering Antivaccination Attitudes," *Proceedings of the National Academy of Sciences* 112, no. 33 (2015): 10321–24.

2. (Emotion) How We Were Persuaded to Reach for the Moon

1. "John F. Kennedy Moon Speech—Rice Stadium," NASA, http://er.jsc.nasa.gov/seh/ricetalk.htm.

2. https://en.wikipedia.org/wiki/We_choose_to_go_to_the_Moon; Jesus Diaz, May 25, 2011, http://gizmodo.com/5805457/kennedys-crazy -moon-speech-and-how-we-could-have-landed-on-the-moon-with-the -soviets; Mike Wall, "The Moon and Man at 50: Why JFK Space Exploration Speech Still Resonates," Space.com, May 25, 2011, http://www.space .com/11774-jfk-speech-moon-exploration-kennedy-congress-50years.html; Mike Wall, "Moon Speech Still Resonates 50 Years Later," Space.com, September 12, 2012, http://www.space.com/17547-jfk-moon-speech -50years-anniversary.html; Excerpt from the Special Message to the

Congress on National Needs, https://www.nasa.gov/vision/space/features
/jfk_speech_text.html#.Vx06MXoXLnY.

3. "John F. Kennedy Moon Speech."

4. Excerpt from the Special Message to the Congress on National Needs,
   https://www.nasa.gov/vision/space/features/jfk_speech_text.html#
   .Vx06MXoXLnY.

5. Susan Cain, *Quiet: The Power of Introverts in a World That Can't Stop Talking* (New York: Broadway Books, 2013), https://www.ted.com/talks
   /susan_cain_the_power_of_introverts?language=en.

6. R. Schmälzle, F. E. Häcker, C. J. Honey, and U. Hasson, "Engaged Listeners: Shared Neural Processing of Powerful Political Speeches," *Social
   Cognition and Affective Neuroscience* 10, no. 8 (August 2015): 1137–43.

7. U. Hasson, Y. Nir, I. Levy, G. Fuhrmann, and R. Malach, "Intersubject
   Synchronization of Cortical Activity During Natural Vision," *Science* 303
   (2004): 1634–40.

8. Lauri Nummenmaa, et al., "Emotions Promote Social Interaction by
   Synchronizing Brain Activity Across Individuals," *Proceedings of the
   National Academy of Sciences* 109, no. 24 (2012): 9599–9604.

9. U. Hasson, A. A. Ghazanfar, B. Galantucci, S. Garrod, and C. Keysers,
   "Brain-to-Brain Coupling: Mechanism for Creating and Sharing a Social
   World," *Trends in Cognitive Sciences* 16, no. 2 (2012): 114–21.

10. U. Hasson, "I Can Make Your Brain Look Like Mine," *Harvard Business
    Review* 88 (2010): 32–33.

11. G. J. Stephens, L. J. Silbert, and U. Hasson, "Speaker-Listener Neural
    Coupling Underlies Successful Communication," *Proceedings of the National
    Academy of Sciences* 107, no. 32 (2010): 14425–30.

12. Lauri Nummenmaa, "Emotional Speech Synchronizes Brains Across Lis-
    teners and Engages Large-Scale Dynamic Brain Networks," *Neuroimage*
    102 (2014): 498–509; Nummenmaa, "Emotions Promote Social Interaction
    by Synchronizing Brain Activity Across Individuals."

13. L. Nummenmaa, J. Hirvonen, R. Parkkola, and J. K. Hietanen, "Is Emo-
    tional Contagion Special? An fMRI Study on Neural Systems for Affective
    and Cognitive Empathy," *Neuroimage* 43, no. 3 (2008), 571–80; S. G. Shamay-
    Tsoory, "The Neural Bases for Empathy," *Neuroscientist* 17, no. 1 (2011): 18–24.

14. S. F. Waters, T. V. West, and W. B. Mendes, "Stress Contagion Physio-
    logical Covariation Between Mothers and Infants," *Psychological Science*
    25, no. 4 (2014): 934–42.

15. A. D. Kramer, J. E. Guillory, and J. T. Hancock, "Experimental Evidence of Massive-Scale Emotional Contagion Through Social Networks," *Proceedings of the National Academy of Sciences* 111, no. 24 (2014): 8788–90.

16. E. Ferrara and Z. Yang, "Measuring Emotional Contagion in Social Media," *PLoS One* 10, no. 11 (2015): e0142390.

17. Steven Levy, "To Demonstrate the Power of Tweets, Twitter's Ad Researchers Turned to Neuroscience. Here's What Happened," backchannel.com, February 5, 2015, https://backchannel.com/this-is-your-brain-on -twitter-cac0725cea2b#.c6mw7aqfc.

18. D. Kahneman, *Thinking, Fast and Slow* (New York: Macmillan, 2011).

19. S. G. Barsade, "The Ripple Effect: Emotional Contagion and Its Influence on Group Behavior," *Administrative Science Quarterly* 47, no. 4 (2002): 644–75.

20. S. V. Shepherd, S. A. Steckenfinger, U. Hasson, and A. A. Ghazanfar, "Human-Monkey Gaze Correlations Reveal Convergent and Divergent Patterns of Movie Viewing," *Current Biology* 20 (2010): 649–56.

21. P. J. Whalen, J. Kagan, R. G. Cook et al., "Human Amygdala Responsivity to Masked Fearful Eye Whites," *Science* 306, no. 5704 (2004): 2061.

3. (Incentives) Should You Scare People into Action?

1. "Surveillance for Foodborne Disease Outbreaks—United States, 1998–2008," *Morbidity and Mortality Weekly Report* 62, no. SS2 (June 2013); Dana Liebelson, "62 Percent of Restaurant Workers Don't Wash Their Hands After Handling Raw Beef," *Mother Jones,* December 13, 2013.

2. Donna Armellino et al., "Using High-Technology to Enforce Low-Technology Safety Measures: The Use of Third-Party Remote Video Auditing and Real-Time Feedback in Healthcare," *Clinical Infectious Diseases* (2011): cir773; Green et al., "Food Worker Hand Washing Practices: An Observation Study," *Journal of Food Protection* 69, no. 10 (2006): 2417–23.

3. Carl P. Borchgrevink, Jaemin Cha, and SeungHyun Kim, "Hand Washing Practices in a College Town Environment," *Journal of Environmental Health* 75, no. 8 (2013): 18–24.

4. Donna Armellino et al., "Using High-Technology to Enforce Low-Technology Safety Measures."

5. Donna Armellino et al., "Replicating Changes in Hand Hygiene in a Surgical Intensive Care Unit with Remote Video Auditing and Feedback," *American Journal of Infection Control* 41, no. 10 (2013): 925–27.

6. Jeremy Bentham, *An Introduction to the Principles of Morals and Legislation* (Oxford: Clarendon Press, 1879); the italics in the second sentence are mine.

7. Wayne A. Hershberger, "An Approach Through the Looking-Glass," *Animal Learning & Behavior* 14, no. 4 (1986): 443–51.

8. Marc Guitart-Masip et al., "Action Controls Dopaminergic Enhancement of Reward Representations," *Proceedings of the National Academy of Sciences* 109, no. 19 (2012): 7511–16.

9. Ibid.

10. Alexander Genevsky and Brian Knutson, "Neural Affective Mechanisms Predict Market-Level Microlending," *Psychological Science* 26, no. 9 (2015): 1411–22.

11. S. H. Bracha, "Freeze, Flight, Fight, Fright, Faint: Adaptationist Perspectives on the Acute Stress Response Spectrum," *CNS Spectrums* 9, no. 9 (2004): 679–85; S. M. Korte, M. K. Jaap, J. C. Wingfield, and B. S. McEwen, "The Darwinian Concept of Stress: Benefits of Allostasis and Costs of Allostatic Load and the Trade-Offs in Health and Disease," *Neuroscience and Biobehavioral Reviews* 29, no. 1 (2005): 3–38.

12. A. E. Power and J. L. McGaugh, "Cholinergic Activation of the Basolateral Amygdala Regulates Unlearned Freezing Behavior in Rats," *Behavioural Brain Research* 134, nos. 1–2 (August 2002): 307–15.

13. Walter Mischel, Yuichi Shoda, and Philip K. Peake, "The Nature of Adolescent Competencies Predicted by Preschool Delay of Gratification," *Journal of Personality and Social Psychology* 54, no. 4 (1988): 687.

14. Joseph W. Kable and Paul W. Glimcher, "An 'As Soon as Possible' Effect in Human Intertemporal Decision Making: Behavioral Evidence and Neural Mechanisms," *Journal of Neurophysiology* 103, no. 5 (2010): 2513–31.

15. Walter Mischel, Yuichi Shoda, and Monica I. Rodriguez, "Delay of Gratification in Children," *Science* 244, no. 4907 (1989): 933–38.

16. Tali Sharot, *The Optimism Bias: A Tour of the Irrationally Positive Brain* (New York: Vintage, 2011); Matthew D. Lieberman, *Social: Why Our Brains Are Wired to Connect* (New York: Oxford University Press, 2013).

17. Celeste Kidd, Holly Palmeri, and Richard N. Aslin, "Rational Snacking: Young Children's Decision-Making on the Marshmallow Task Is Moderated by Beliefs About Environmental Reliability," *Cognition* 126, no. 1 (2013): 109–114.

4. (Agency) How You Obtain Power by Letting Go

1. Center for Disease Control and Prevention, "Leading Causes of Death," http://www.cdc.gov/nchs/fastats/leading-causes-of-death.htm.

2. "Phobia List—The Ultimate List of Phobias and Fears," http://www.fearof .net.

3. R. L. Langley, "Animal-Related Fatalities in the United States: An Update," *Wilderness and Environmental Medicine* 16 (2005): 67–74.

4. Mark Borden, "Hollywood's Rogue Mogul: How Terminator Director McG Is Blowing Up the Movie Business," *Fast Company Magazine*, May 2009.

5. Harold Mass, "The Odds are 11 Million to 1 That You Die in a Plane Crash," *The Week*, July 8, 2013, http://theweek.com/articles/462449/odds -are-11-million-1-that-youll-die-plane-crash.

6. Borden, "Hollywood's Rogue Mogul."

7. Chris Matthews, "Here's How Much Tax Cheats Cost the U.S. Government a Year," *Fortune*, April 29, 2016, http://fortune.com/2016/04/29/tax -evasion-cost.

8. C. P. Lamberton, J. E. De Neve, and M. I. Norton, "Eliciting Taxpayer Preferences Increases Tax Compliance," working paper, 2014; available at SSRN 2365751.

9. L. A. Leotti, S. S. Iyengar, and K. N. Ochsner, "Born to Choose: The Origins and Value of the Need for Control," *Trends in Cognitive Sciences* 14, no. 10 (2010): 457–63.

10. L. A. Leotti and M. R. Delgado, "The Inherent Reward of Choice," *Psychological Science* 22, no. 10 (2011): 1310–18, doi.org/10.1177/095679761141 7005; L. A. Leotti and M. R. Delgado, "The Value of Exercising Control over Monetary Gains and Losses," *Psychological Science* 25, no. 2 (2014): 596–604, doi.org/10.1177/0956797613514589.

11. N. J. Bown, D. Read, and B. Summers, "The Lure of Choice," *Journal of Behavioral Decision Making* 16, no. 4 (2003): 297.

12. Stephen C. Voss and M. J. Homzie, "Choice as a Value," *Psychological Reports* 26, no. 3 (1970): 912–14.

13. A. C. Catania and T. Sagvolden, "Preference for Free Choice Over Forced Choice in Pigeons," *Journal of the Experimental Analysis of Behavior* 34, no. 1 (1980): 77–86; A. C. Catania, "Freedom of Choice: A Behavioral Analysis," *Psychology of Learning and Motivation* 14 (1981): 97–145.

14. Bown et al., "Lure."

15. Sheena S. Iyengar and Mark R. Lepper, "When Choice Is Demotivating: Can One Desire Too Much of a Good Thing?," *Journal of Personality and Social Psychology* 79, no. 6 (2000): 995.

16. http://www.onemint.com/.

17. Manshu, "Why I Pick Stocks," *The Digerati Life*, April 28, 2009, http://www.thedigeratilife.com/blog/index.php/2009/04/28/pick-stocks-choosing-individual-stocks-mutual-funds/.

18. Laurent Barras, Olivier Scaillet, and Russ Wermers, "False Discoveries in Mutual Fund Performance: Measuring Luck in Estimated Alphas," *Journal of Finance* 65, no. 1 (2010): 179–216.

19. D. Owens, Z. Grossman, and R. Fackler, "The Control Premium: A Preference for Payoff Autonomy," *American Economic Journal: Microeconomics* 6, no. 4 (2014): 138–61, doi.org/10.1257/mic.6.4.138.

20. Sebastian Bobadilla-Suarez, Cass R. Sunstein, and Tali Sharot, "The Intrinsic Value of Control: The Propensity to Under-delegate in the Face of Potential Gains and Losses," *Journal of Risk and Uncertainty* (forthcoming).

21. D. H. Shapiro Jr., C. E. Schwartz, and J. A. Astin, "Controlling Ourselves, Controlling Our World: Psychology's Role in Understanding Positive and Negative Consequences of Seeking and Gaining Control," *American Psychologist* 51, no. 12 (1996): 1213.

22. Ibid.

23. Judith Rodin and Ellen J. Langer, "Long-Term Effects of a Control-Relevant Intervention with the Institutionalized Aged," *Journal of Personality and Social Psychology* 35, no. 12 (1977): 897.

24. Michael I. Norton, Daniel Mochon, and Dan Ariely, "The 'IKEA Effect': When Labor Leads to Love," Harvard Business School Marketing Unit Working Paper 11-091 (2011).

25. Raphael Koster et al., "How Beliefs About Self-Creation Inflate Value in the Human Brain," *Frontiers in Human Neuroscience* 9 (2015).

26. Daniel Wolpert, "The Real Reason for Brains," TED, http://www.ted.com/talks/daniel_wolpert_the_real_reason_for_brains.

27. E. A. Patall, H. Cooper, and J. C. Robinson, "The Effects of Choice on Intrinsic Motivation and Related Outcomes: A Meta-Analysis of Research Findings," *Psychological Bulletin* 134, no. 2 (2008): 270.

Further Reading

Sharot, T., B. De Martino, and R. J. Dolan. "How Choice Reveals and Shapes Expected Hedonic Outcome." *Journal of Neuroscience* 29, no. 12 (2009): 3760–65. doi.org/10.1523/JNEUROSCI.4972-08.2009.

Sharot, T., T. Shiner, and R. J. Dolan. "Experience and Choice Shape Expected Aversive Outcomes." *Journal of Neuroscience* 30, no. 27 (2010): 9209–15. doi.org/10.1523/JNEUROSCI.4770-09.2010.

Sharot, T., C. M. Velasquez, and R. J. Dolan. "Do Decisions Shape Preference? Evidence from Blind Choice." *Psychological Science* 21, no. 9 (2010): 1231–35. doi.org/10.1177/0956797610379235.

Thompson, Suzanne C. "Illusions of Control: How We Overestimate Our Personal Influence." *Current Directions in Psychological Science* 8, no. 6 (1999): 187–90.

Langer, E., and J. Rodin. "The Effects of Choice and Enhanced Personal Responsibility for the Aged: A Field Experiment in an Institutional Setting." *Journal of Personality and Social Psychology* 34 (1976): 191–98.

Schulz, Richard. "Effects of Control and Predictability on the Physical and Psychological Well-Being of the Institutionalized Aged." *Journal of Personality and Social Psychology* 33, no. 5 (1976): 563.

Cockburn, Jeffrey, Anne G. E. Collins, and Michael J. Frank. "A Reinforcement Learning Mechanism Responsible for the Valuation of Free Choice." *Neuron* 83, no. 3 (2014): 551–57.

5. (Curiosity) What Do People Really Want to Know?

1. "How Virgin America Got Six Million People to Watch a Flight Safety Video Without Stepping on a Plane," Digital Synopsis, https://digitalsyno psis.com/advertising/virgin-america-safety-dance-video/.

2. Ed Felten, "Harvard Business School Boots 119 Applicants for 'Hacking' into Admissions Site," Freedom to Tinker, March 9, 2005; https://freedom -to-tinker.com/2005/03/09/harvard-business-school-boots-119 -applicants-hacking-admissions-site/; Jay Lindsay, "College Admissions Sites Breached: Business Schools Reject Applicants Who Sought Sneak Peek," Associated Press, March 9, 2005.

3. Yael Niv and Stephanie Chan, "On the Value of Information and Other Rewards," *Nature Neuroscience* 14, no. 9 (2011): 1095.

4. Ibid.

5. Ethan S. Bromberg-Martin and Okihide Hikosaka, "Midbrain Dopamine Neurons Signal Preference for Advance Information About Upcoming Rewards," *Neuron* 63, vol. 1 (2009): 119–26; Ethan S. Bromberg-Martin and Okihide Hikosaka, "Lateral Habenula Neurons Signal Errors in the Prediction of Reward Information," *Nature Neuroscience* 14, no. 9 (2011): 1209–16.

6. R. L. Bennett, *Testing for Huntington Disease: Making an Informed Choice* Medical Genetics (Seattle: University of Washington Medical Center).

7. Bettina Meiser and Stewart Dunn, "Psychological Impact of Genetic Testing for Huntington's Disease: An Update of the Literature," *Journal of Neurology, Neurosurgery and Psychiatry* 69, no. 5 (2000): 574–78.

8. Andrew Caplin and Kfir Eliaz, "AIDS Policy and Psychology: A Mechanism-Design Approach," *RAND Journal of Economics* 34, no. 4 (2003): 631–46.

9. C. Lerman, C. Hughes, S. Lemon, et al., "What You Don't Know Can Hurt You: Adverse Psychological Effects in Members of BRCA1-Linked and BRCA2-Linked Families Who Decline Genetic Testing," *Journal of Clinical Oncology* 16 (1998): 1650–54.

10. Niklas Karlsson, George Loewenstein, and Duane Seppi, "The Ostrich Effect: Selective Attention to Information," *Journal of Risk and Uncertainty* 38, no. 2 (2009): 95–15.

11. Ibid.

12. Emily Oster, Ira Shoulson, and E. Dorsey, "Optimal Expectations and Limited Medical Testing: Evidence from Huntington Disease," *American Economic Review* 103, no. 2 (2013): 804–30.

13. James R. Averill and Miriam Rosenn, "Vigilant and Nonvigilant Coping Strategies and Psychophysiological Stress Reactions During the Anticipation of Electric Shock," *Journal of Personality and Social Psychology* 23, no. 1 (1972): 128.

14. Paige Weaver, "Don't Torture Yourself," *Paige Weaver* (blog), April 20, 2013.

15. Kristin Cashore, *This Is My Secret* (blog), 2008.

16. "Dick Cheney's Suite Demands," *The Smoking Gun*, March 22, 2006, http://www.thesmokinggun.com/documents/crime/dick-cheneys-suite -demands.

Further Reading

Zentall, Thomas R., and Jessica Stagner. "Maladaptive Choice Behaviour by Pigeons: An Animal Analogue and Possible Mechanism for Gambling

(Sub-Optimal Human Decision-Making Behaviour)." *Proceedings of the Royal Society B: Biological Sciences* 278, no. 1709 (2011): 1203–08.

Babu, Deepti. "Is Access to Predictive Genetic Testing for Huntington's Disease a Problem?" *HD Buzz*. April 23, 2013.

Blanchard, Tommy C., Benjamin Y. Hayden, and Ethan S. Bromberg-Martin. "Orbitofrontal Cortex Uses Distinct Codes for Different Choice Attributes in Decisions Motivated by Curiosity." *Neuron* (January 22, 2015).

6: (State) What Happens to Minds Under Threat?

1. David K. Shipler, "More Schoolgirls in West Bank Fall Sick," *New York Times*, April 4, 1983.
2. Robert Sapolsky, *Stress and Your Body* (The Great Courses, 2013).
3. Neil Garrett, Ana María González-Garzón, Lucy Foulkes, Liat Levita, and Tali Sharot, "Updating Beliefs Under Threat." In preparation.
4. Anne Ball, "Fear of Terrorism Spreads Far Beyond Paris," Learning English, November 18, 2015, http://learningenglish.voanews.com/a/paris-terrorist-attack-causes-fear-worldwide/3063741.html.
5. http://www.pressreader.com/.
6. Avinash Kunnath, "Jeff Tedford: Where Things Went Wrong," http://www.pacifictakes.com/cal-bears/2012/11/16/3648578/jeff-tedford-california-golden-bears-head-coach-history.
7. Ibid.
8. Ibid.
9. Avinash Kunnath, "Coach Tedford the Playcaller: Part I," http://www.californiagoldenblogs.com/2009/4/7/824135/coach-tedford-the-playcaller-part-i.
10. Brian Burke, "Are NFL Coaches Too Timid?," http://archive.advanced footballanalytics.com/2009/05/are-nfl-coaches-too-timid.html.
11. Chris Brown, "Smart Football," http://smartfootball.blogspot.com/2009/02/conservative-and-risky-football.html.
12. Greg Garber, "Chang Refused to Lose Twenty Years Ago," ESPN.com, May 20, 2009.
13. Ibid.
14. Steven Pye, "How Michael Chang Defeated Ivan Lendl at the French Open in 1989," *Guardian*, http://www.theguardian.com/sport/that-1980s-sports-blog/2013/may/21/michael-chang-ivan-lendl-french-open-1989.
15. Paul Gittings, "Chang's 'Underhand' Tactics Stunned Lendl and Made

Tennis History," CNN, http://edition.cnn.com/2012/06/08/sport/tennis/tennis-chang-underhand-service-french-open-lin/index.html.

16. Ibid.

17. Pye, "How Michael Chang Defeated Ivan Lendl at the French Open in 1989."

18. Gittings, "Chang's 'Underhand' Tactics Stunned Lendl and Made Tennis History."

19. Pye, "How Michael Chang Defeated Ivan Lendl at the French Open in 1989."

20. L. Guiso, P. Sapienza, and L. Zingales, "Time Varying Risk Aversion," NBER Working Paper no. w19284 (2013); available at http://www.nber.org/papers/w19284.

21. R. M. Heilman, L. G. Crişan, D. Houser, M. Miclea, and A. C. Miu, "Emotion Regulation and Decision Making Under Risk and Uncertainty," *Emotion* 10 (2010): 257–65.

22. Kenneth T. Kishida et al., "Implicit Signals in Small Group Settings and Their Impact on the Expression of Cognitive Capacity and Associated Brain Responses," *Philosophical Transactions of the Royal Society B: Biological Sciences* 367, no. 1589 (2012): 704–16.

23. Gregory J. Quirk and Jennifer S. Beer, "Prefrontal Involvement in the Regulation of Emotion: Convergence of Rat and Human Studies," *Current Opinion in Neurobiology* 16, no. 6 (2006): 723–27.

24. A. Ross Otto, Stephen M. Fleming, and Paul W. Glimcher, "Unexpected but Incidental Positive Outcomes Predict Real-World Gambling," *Psychological Science* (2016): 0956797615618366.

7. (Others, Part I) Why Do Babies Love iPhones?

1. Jeanna Bryner, "Good or Bad, Baby Names Have Long-Lasting Effects," *Live Science*, June 13, 2010.

2. Rob Siltanen, "The Real Story Behind Apple's 'Think Different' Campaign," *Forbes*, December 14, 2011.

3. Ibid.

4. Albert Bandura, Dorothea Ross, and Sheila A. Ross, "Imitation of Film-Mediated Aggressive Models," *Journal of Abnormal and Social Psychology* 66, no. 1 (1963): 3.

5. Caroline J. Charpentier et al., "The Brain's Temporal Dynamics from a Collective Decision to Individual Action," *Journal of Neuroscience* 34, no. 17 (2014): 5816–23.

6. Bryan Alexander, "*Sideways* at 10: Still Not Drinking Any Merlot?," USA TODAY, October 6, 2014, http://www.usatoday.com/story/life/movies/2014/10/06/sideways-killed-merlot/15901489/.

7. Juanjuan, Zhang, "The Sound of Silence: Observational Learning in the U.S. Kidney Market," *Marketing Science* 29, no. 2 (2010): 315–35.

8. Lev Muchnik, Sinan Aral, and Sean J. Taylor, "Social Influence Bias: A Randomized Experiment," *Science* 341, no. 6146 (2013): 647–51.

9. Micah Edelson, Tali Sharot, R. J. Dolan, and Y. Dudai, "Following the Crowd: Brain Substrates of Long-Term Memory Conformity," *Science* 333 no. 6038 (2011): 108–111.

10. Joseph LeDoux, *The Emotional Brain: The Mysterious Underpinnings of Emotional Life* (New York: Simon and Schuster, 1998).

11. Heinrich Klüver and Paul C. Bucy, "Preliminary Analysis of Functions of the Temporal Lobes in Monkeys," *Archives of Neurology and Psychiatry* 42, no. 6 (December 1939): 979–1000.

12. Kevin C. Bickart et al., "Amygdala Volume and Social Network Size in Humans," *Nature Neuroscience* 14, no. 2 (2011): 163–64.

13. Edelson et al, "Following the Crowd."

14. Micah Edelson, Y. Dudai, R. J. Dolan, and Tali Sharot, "Brain Substrates of Recovery from Misleading Influence," *Journal of Neuroscience* 34, no. 23 (2014): 7744–53.

15. Christophe P. Chamley, *Rational Herds: Economic Models of Social Learning* (Cambridge, UK: Cambridge University Press, 2004).

16. Albert Bandura, "Influence of Models' Reinforcement Contingencies on the Acquisition of Imitative Responses," *Journal of Personality and Social Psychology* 1, no. 6 (1965): 589.

17. Kyoko Yoshida et al., "Social Error Monitoring in Macaque Frontal Cortex," *Nature Neuroscience* 15, no. 9 (2012): 1307–12.

18. Wolfram Schultz, Peter Dayan, and P. Read Montague, "A Neural Substrate of Prediction and Reward," *Science* 275, no. 5306 (1997): 1593–99.

19. Christopher J. Burke et al., "Neural Mechanisms of Observational Learning," *Proceedings of the National Academy of Sciences* 107, no. 32 (2010): 14431–36.

20. Paul A. Howard-Jones et al., "The Neural Mechanisms of Learning from Competitors," *Neuroimage* 53, no. 2 (2010): 790–99.

21. Rebecca Saxe and Nancy Kanwisher, "People Thinking About Thinking People: The Role of the Temporo-Parietal Junction in 'Theory of Mind,'" *Neuroimage* 19, no. 4 (2003): 1835–42.

22. De Martino, Benedetto, et al, "In the Mind of the Market: Theory of Mind Biases Value Computation During Financial Bubbles," *Neuron* 79, no. 6 (2013): 1222–31.

8. (Others, Part II) Is "Unanimous" as Reassuring as It Sounds?

1. "Man Booker Winner's Debut Novel Rejected Nearly Eighty Times," *Guardian*, October 14, 2015.
2. "Revealed: The Eight-Year-Old Girl Who Saved Harry Potter," *Independent*, July 2, 2005.
3. Ibid.
4. Francis Galton, "Vox Populi (the Wisdom of Crowds)," *Nature* 75 (1907): 450–51.
5. James Surowiecki, *The Wisdom of Crowds* (New York: Anchor, 2005).
6. Micah Edelson, Tali Sharot, R. J. Dolan, and Y. Dudai, "Following the Crowd: Brain Substrates of Long-Term Memory Conformity," *Science* 333, no. 6038 (2011): 108–111.
7. Julia A. Minson and Jennifer S. Mueller, "The Cost of Collaboration: Why Joint Decision Making Exacerbates Rejection of Outside Information," *Psychological Science* 23, no. 3 (2012): 219–24.
8. Edward Vul and Harold Pashler, "Measuring the Crowd Within Probabilistic Representations Within Individuals," *Psychological Science* 19, no. 7 (2008): 645–47.
9. Ali Mahmoodi et al., "Equality Bias Impairs Collective Decision-Making Across Cultures," *Proceedings of the National Academy of Sciences* 112, no. 12 (2015): 3835–40.
10. Tali Sharot, *The Optimism Bias: A Tour of the Irrationally Positive Brain* (New York: Vintage, 2011).
11. Michale L. Kalish, Thomas L. Griffiths, and Stephan Lewandowsky, "Iterated Learning: Intergenerational Knowledge Transmission Reveals Inductive Biases," *Psychonomic Bulletin & Review* 14, no. 2 (2007): 288–94.
12. Ibid.
13. Ibid.
14. Kalish, "Iterated Learning."
15. Mahmoodi, "Equality Bias."
16. Shane Frederick, "Cognitive Reflection and Decision Making," *Journal of Economic Perspectives*, 19, no. 4 (2005): 25–42, doi:10.1257/089533005775196732, retrieved December 1, 2015.

17. Prelec, Drazen, H. Sebastian Seung, and John McCoy. "Finding Truth even if the Crowd Is Wrong," Technical report, Working paper, MIT, 2013.

9. The Future of Influence?

1. A. Belfer-Cohen and N. Goren-Inbar, "Cognition and Communication in the Levantine Lower Palaeolithic," *World Archaeology* 26 (1994): 144–57, doi: 10.1080/00438243.1994.9980269.

2. F. L. Coolidge and T. Wynn, "Working Memory, Its Executive Functions, and the Emergence of Modern Thinking," *Cambridge Archaeological Journal* 15 (2005): 5–26, doi: 10.1017/S0959774305000016.

3. Peter T. Daniels, "The Study of Writing Systems," in *The World's Writing Systems*, ed. William Bright and Peter T. Daniels (New York: Oxford University Press, 1996).

4. Lucien Febvre and Henri-Jean Martin, *The Coming of the Book: The Impact of Printing, 1450–1800* (London: New Left Books, 1976), quoted in Benedict Anderson, *Comunidades Imaginadas: Reflexiones Sobre el Origen y la Difusión del Nacionalismo* (Mexico: Fondo de Cultura Económica, 1993).

5. P. K. Bondyopadhyay, "Guglielmo Marconi: The Father of Long Distance Radio Communication—An Engineer's Tribute," paper, European Microwave Conference, September 4, 1995.

6. "Current Topics and Events," *Nature* 115 (April 4, 1925): 505–06, doi: 10.1038/115504a0.

7. Mitchell Stephens, "History of Television," *Grolier Encyclopedia*, https://www.nyu.edu/classes/stephens/History%20of%20Television%20page.htm.

8. "The first ISP," Indra.com, August 13, 1992; archived from the original on March 5, 2016, retrieved on October 17, 2015.

9. J. Hawks, "How Has the Human Brain Evolved?," *Scientific American* (2013): 6.

10. J. K. Rilling and T. R. Insel, "The Primate Neocortex in Comparative Perspective Using Magnetic Resonance Imaging," *Journal of Human Evolution* 37, no. 2 (1999): 191–223.

11. U. Hasson, A. A. Ghazanfar, B. Galantucci, S. Garrod, and C. Keysers, "Brain-to-Brain Coupling: A Mechanism for Creating and Sharing a Social World," *Trends in Cognitive Sciences* 16, no. 2 (2012): 114–21.

12. Miguel Pais-Vieira et al., "A Brain-to-Brain Interface for Real-Time Sharing of Sensorimotor Information," *Scientific Reports* 3 (2013).

13. Ian Sample, "Brain-to-Brain Interface Lets Rats Share Information via

Internet," *Guardian*, March 1, 2013, https://www.theguardian.com/science/2013/feb/28/brains-rats-connected-share-information.

14. Daniel Engber, "The Neurologist Who Hacked His Brain—and Almost Lost His Mind," *Wired*, January 26, 2016, http://www.wired.com/2016/01/phil-kennedy-mind-control-computer/.

15. Ibid.

16. Seung-Schik Yoo et al., "Non-Invasive Brain-to-Brain Interface (BBI): Establishing Functional Links Between Two Brains," *PLoS One* 8, no. 4 (2013): e60410.

17. Sebastian Anthony, "Harvard Creates Brain-to-Brain Interface, Allows Humans to Control Other Animals with Thoughts Alone," Extremetech, July 31, 2013, http://www.extremetech.com/extreme/162678-harvard-creates-brain-to-brain-interface-allows-humans-to-control-other-animals-with-thoughts-alone.

18. Seung-Schik Yoo et al., "Non-Invasive Brain-to-Brain Interface (BBI): Establishing Functional Links Between Two Brains," *PLoS One* 8, no. 4 (2013): e60410.

19. Charles Q. Choi, "Quadriplegic Woman Moves Robot Arm with Her Mind," *Live Science*, December 17, 2012, http://www.livescience.com/25600-quadriplegic-mind-controlled-prosthetic.html.

20. Abby Phillip, "A Paralyzed Woman Flew an F-35 Fighter Jet in a Simulator Using Only Her Mind," *The Washington Post*, March 3, 2015, https://www.washingtonpost.com/news/speaking-of-science/wp/2015/03/03/a-paralyzed-woman-flew-a-f-35-fighter-jet-in-a-simulator-using-only-her-mind/.

21. Rajesh P. N. Rao et al., "A Direct Brain-to-Brain Interface in Humans," *PLoS One* 9, no. 11 (2014): e111332.

22. Doree Armstrong and Michelle Ma, "Researcher Controls Colleague's Motions in First Human Brain-to-Brain Interface," *UW Today*, August 27, 2013, http://www.washington.edu/news/2013/08/27/researcher-controls-colleagues-motions-in-1st-human-brain-to-brain-interface/.

23. W. B. Scoville and B. Milner, "Loss of Recent Memory After Bilateral Hippocampal Lesions," *Journal of Neurology, Neurosurgery, and Psychiatry* February 20, no. 1 (1957): 11–21.

24. J. M. Harlow, "Passage of an Iron Rod Through the Head," *Journal of Neuropsychiatry and Clinical Neurosciences* 11, no. 2 (1999): 281–83.

Acknowledgments

In many ways the idea of *The Influential Mind* originated from readers of my previous book, *The Optimism Bias: A Tour of the Irrationally Positive Brain*. I often received e-mails from readers who wanted to know how my research informed the way they should communicate with others: their children, spouses, employees, and clients. What were the implications for education, politics, business, and social media, people asked. These questions resonated with me. At the time I was building a research group of my own and starting a new family, so the question of how my behavior was influencing others—members of my team and my family—was constantly on my mind. I have been studying the human brain for many years in the lab, so I began looking at the data I had acquired, and that of my colleagues, for insight.

For the evidence presented in this book I owe a huge thank-you to my students at the Affective Brain Lab, who tirelessly run experiments to better understand human behavior. The studies presented in this book are the work of Neil Garrett, Caroline Charpentier, Christina Moutsiana, Filip Gesiarz, Sebastian Bobadilla-Suarez, Ana Maria Gonzalez, Stephanie Lazzaro, Raphael Koster, and Andreas Kappes. My curiosity in many of the ideas described in this book was triggered by my brilliant collaborators. In particular, Micah Edelson, Jan-Emmanuel De Neve, Marc Guitart-Masip, Michael Norton, Benedetto De Martino, Yadin Dudai, Ray Dolan, Ethan Bromberg-Martin, Bahador Baharami, Drazen Prelec, and Cass Sunstein. Micah, Benedetto, Jan, Marc, Andreas, Stephanie, and Cass kindly read early versions of this book and provided insightful comments. My many conversations with Cass helped structure the book into its current form, for which I am grateful. My friends Tamara Shiner and Amir Doron read and commented on drafts of the book. Amir also pointed me to many of the stories you can find within these pages.

My exceptional agents—Heather Schroder (Compass Talent) and Sophie Lambert (Conville and Walsh)—went above and beyond to ensure my research would reach others. This was made possible by my editors—Serena Jones (Henry Holt) and Tim Whiting (Little, Brown)—who, with experience, talent, and patience, went through early versions of this book until *The Influential Mind* was formed. The illustrations in the book are the brilliant work of Lisa Brennan. The final product was shaped by them all.

I first pitched the idea of the book to Tim Whiting two weeks after my daughter, Livia, was born. During the next three years of writing this book I had the privilege of witnessing her, and her brother Leo, who joined us soon after, grow into talking, thinking, human beings. My interactions with them influenced my thinking and are interleaved in this book. I am hugely grateful for their presence and love in my life. I owe a great deal to all the others who love and care for them, influencing their characters in positive ways. In particular, my parents and in-laws who play, sing, and read, and provide wonderful role models. My extraordinary husband, Josh McDermott, was present every step of the way providing love, support, and advice. I could always rely on him for motivating pep talks whenever obstacles or doubts raised their head. This book is dedicated to him.

Index

—◇◇◇—